THIS HOUSE IS CONDEMNED

Other Titles by David Haskins

Reclamation

THIS HOUSE IS CONDEMNED

David Haskins

**WOLSAK
& WYNN**

Interior and cover design: Dawn Kresan
Author photograph: Jason Haskins
Typset in Adobe Garamond Pro
Printed by Coach House Printing Company Toronto, Canada

The publisher gratefully acknowledges the support of the Canada Council for the Arts, the Ontario Arts Council and the Canada Book Fund.

Wolsak and Wynn Publishers Ltd.
280 James Street North
Hamilton, ON
Canada L8R 2L3

LIBRARY AND ARCHIVES CANADA CATALOGUING IN PUBLICATION

Haskins, David, 1944-, author
This house is condemned / David Haskins.

ISBN 978-1-894987-78-3 (PBK.)

  1. Haskins, David, 1944– . 2. Authors, Canadian (English) –
20th century – Biography – Anecdotes. 3. Ontario, Lake (N.Y. and Ont.) – Biography – Anecdotes. I. Title.

PS8565.A725T55 2013   C814'.54   C2013-906958-5

For Shirl

Table of Contents

Introduction

Memory, history, interpretation, fact and fiction — these are the elements of memoir. Selective memory, personal history, subjective interpretation, verifiable fact and imaginative fiction. Each has its window on truth.

A memoir is said to be a true story. Of the many variations on a memoir, two chosen for this book involve events that actually happened, as I remember them, and events that never happened, but sprung from some kernel of truth in the circumstances that generated them.

The former, those accounts of what actually happened, are filtered through the selection process of memory and an aesthetic sensibility. The latter are works of fiction and poetry which originate in some experience that was mine.

The obvious truth is that we cannot recreate life as it was. There is no time machine but in fiction, no innocence but in the first time. We have changed in the interim. What we remember is what we think we remember. What is important to us depends on what has happened to us in the meantime. By the time this revision, this remembrance, reaches the reader and tries to insert itself into the reader's experience, which is not the author's, it arrives as a pile of fallen Lego the reader must rebuild according to his or her own instructions.

Some of the Lego blocks that occasioned these pieces are: a pile of old letters, an anecdote, a surrealistic dream, a father's gift to his son, overheard conversations, a sleeping dog in the street, the death of a friend and something a photographer once told me.

When the spur that inspired the author is no more than a peg to hang a story on, or an image to begin a poem's metaphorical exploration, the conventions of the form take over. What matters to the reader, I think, is the consistency and force of the story or poem, not the accurate reproduction of phenomena behind it. What moves us, sometimes even to action, is not the unordered events of life, but the stories those events generate, often in the hands of artists. In this revisioning, the criterion of truth is inside the story, not in some prior occurrence of events. If a memoir is to be a true story, then its truth in my version is its story.

My life has not been extraordinary. I celebrate triumphs, mourn losses, laugh at foibles and stew over regrets, much as anyone does. In this book, I have collected essays, stories and poems that reflect parts of my life as I have reconstructed them because they are valuable to me. I want these pieces to stand on their own because they make for a good read.

Section One

In Place

"Live all you can; it's a mistake not to."
— Strether, in Henry James's *The Ambassadors*

"Where are you off to?" my mother asked as I headed out the back door with my new claw hammer and a box of 4" Ardox spiral nails I had bought from old man Wilcox at Wilcox's Hardware with the week's cherry-picking money.

"Down to the lake," I said.

"Well, don't smash your fingers with that thing," she warned.

Not "Don't drown," or "Watch out for the undertow," or "Who's going with you?" I was free to explore, come what may, my nine-year-old sense of self-preservation trusted to protect me from harm.

Always a canvas for moving light, Lake Ontario never takes on the deep inky blue-black or steel grey of the heaving Atlantic that bore us during our crossing in 1953. Depending on the cloud cover, the lake's hues range from bands of luminescent tropical aqua and bruised purple on summer evenings, to the mirror grey of still water at first light and the burnt orange of a sunset, to clay brown when the north November gales churn the muddy bottom. Clarity and color can change as quickly as a squall can strike.

In the mid-Atlantic, my ship, the Cunard liner *Ascania*, carried a boy toward uncharted places. The bow gave no hint of a destination in the open ocean ahead; the stern pulled a road of white water stretching back to the horizon my family had left behind. Off the starboard rail, I thought I could see the curvature of the earth, the impossible finiteness of this huge adventure I was caught up in.

This Great Lake, however, was only partly contained by the shore where I stood and the refineries and apartment blocks across from me. A thin cord of lights rimmed the western curve of the Golden Horseshoe. The far coastline beckoned, testing my courage, the Toronto skyscrapers calling "Come on, Marilyn Bell did it." Murderous ten-foot swells lurk somewhere between there and here, invisible to the dreamer standing on the shore.

A non-swimmer, sometimes I would set out for Toronto on an inner-tube accompanied on one side by my father and on the other by Kela, our "leader of the wolf pack" Alsatian, who usually got tired and turned back a paddle or two before me.

Anyone who lives within sight of a body of water knows what it means to be happily preoccupied with surfaces. Big as this lake is, the eighth largest freshwater body in North America, we saw only its face and the vessels it carried, never those it buried. Long freighters lined up like boxcars waiting to step up the canal to Lake Erie and beyond after ice breakup. Tall ships crewed by lucky student sailors glided far out under full sail towards the Port Colborne regatta. A flotilla of salmon boats peppered the still water during the spring derby. The summer traffic of pleasure craft followed: speedboats, outboards pulling skiers, catamarans used as deck bars, sailboats and the odd kayak or canoe raking the flat water close to shore. Once, the Royal yacht *Britannia* steamed toward the Welland Canal as I waited with my father on the observation deck at Lock 3, hoping for a brief glimpse of royalty.

What lay beneath the lake was the stuff of tall tales. I was morbidly intrigued by what the darkness harbored or what lay in wait inside this fourteen-thousand-year-old hole in the ground. Dark skeletons were said to travel a submerged road fifteen miles from Grimsby to Jordan. A small plane crashed and sank, its drowned pilot's eyes sucked out by lamprey eels. On those days when the lake and sky were white, I dreamed of a ghostly galleon rising up from the depths and coming for me. Each story began with a seed of truth behind the tale. Lake-front roads still fall away, light aircraft do go down from time to time, and there is talk about raising the *Hamilton* and the *Scourge*, sunken schooners from the War of 1812.

I wrote my summers on the margin between land and inland sea. Here, the grey pebbles and sharp sand were cluttered with waterlogged driftwood for lamps and gardens; shards of clam shells; treasures of red, blue and green glass whose edges were frosted white by the blast of water and grit; float stones for target practice kindly jettisoned from furnaces of passing ships; half-bricks drilled out and smoothed round to look like donuts that might fool our parents; stones like baseballs striped with green mica, pink and white quartz or fool's gold.

Daily, I witnessed the catalogue of life the lake embraced. A loon's morning warble in the fog. Hunter kingfisher. The screaming wail of gulls. Cormorants. Cleanup crows. Skittering sandpipers. Muskrats in the creek banks. Garter snakes. Painted turtles with paintbox patterns on the underside of the plastron. Two-foot-wide snapping turtles whose beaks could snap a shovel handle and whose jagged carapaces could shred a human hand. In the elm tree, a Baltimore oriole's suspended sack gathered its spherical eggs, which could have rolled out of a more conventional nest. Someone had draped an ancient carp carcass over a grape post by its gill, its tail bones brushing the ground.

On a still morning in June, a school of carp cruised past me in a V as perfect as the flight pattern of geese, their dorsal fins cutting the silver surface, each one trailing its own rippling V to echo their formation. They were headed for a shallow creek where they would spawn, shoulder to shoulder so tight I could pick them out of the water by hand.

In the July heat, I raked and gathered up wheelbarrow loads of stinking shad to fertilize our vegetable garden. The fungus-chunked shiners embedded in the matted, sun-baked algae crunched when I walked on them, on days when there was no other passage but their graveyard carpet. Since the banning of phosphates from detergents, fewer of them die, but even now in 2013, the many unknown compounds formed by known chemical wastes threaten the health of the lake and its society.

Edges, ridges, divides. These were my narrow playground. While my friends splashed about fearlessly in the surf, for me every footing was a matter of life and death. The rocky bottom fell away sharply from the water's edge. A few steps out, I was up to my neck. Then I panicked, afraid to lift a foot lest my body tip either forward or backward, forcing my face or head down into the water, with no way to right myself. My heart racing and adrenalin pumping, I held my breath, shifted my foot an inch toward the shore and tested my way to safety. I could not admit my fear of drowning to my friends, who, busy with their own fun, never noticed my plight.

I used the hammer and nails I had bought to build a raft from washed-up barn timbers, logs and oil drums. It measured about six feet square, with a lodgepole pine mast and an old couch arm for the bridge. I found a peeled staff, also about six feet, which I thought would do for a punting pole. I took my first trial voyage on a morning when nobody was around, so I would not have to admit defeat in the very possible event that the thing sank. I pried it into the water and flopped aboard. It floated. Too easily. In a matter of a minute, the raft drifted out of pole depth. With punting no longer an option, I frantically flailed with my pole as a useless paddle. Slowly, the raft began to spin. Toronto came into view.

I pulled out the pole, slumped against the bridge and gazed up at the limp shirt I had thought would make a fine sail. Imperceptibly slowly, the thin current carried me along like flotsam. Even though I couldn't swim, it didn't occur to me to fear drowning on this occasion. I was, however, deathly afraid of not getting back home in time for supper, or in my worst imaginings, of drifting away and not ever being found. Either case would mean that my mother was right to have worried about the hammer and nails.

I scanned the beach one last time and lay down on the rough boards. A lone, lazy cloud commiserated with me. I hardly noticed the gentle *tap … tap …* of timbers against the rocks of Skipper Jones's irrigation pier. I had drifted a quarter-mile down the shore before coming to rest, an anticlimactic end to my Huckleberry escapade.

Wild grapevines wound about the Dutch elm branches, strong enough to jump onto from the top of the cliff and swing out over the beach with a good Tarzan yell. Tommy Whitelaw could drop into the lake from those vines. I settled for a surer footing on dry land, letting myself down hand over hand, like a fireman. Firemen were never called when the farmer lit up the side of the cliff where the winter prunings and uprooted orchard trees and even the odd tire had been tipped. This annual ritual of burning could have warned ships by its blaze.

I further practised my building skills on a mud hut cut into the clay bank of the creek that ran by our house and fed into the lake. I made the roof from the old raft boards salvaged after the drifting episode and supported it on two stolen grape posts. My friends and I started a clubhouse, which had a flagpole with a red rag nailed to it (everything I constructed had a flagpole). We devised a secret handshake and saved Cracker Jack rings, which had to be worn at meetings, where we plotted our adventures and played marbles and traded cards. I don't remember what we called ourselves, but we lasted about three weeks.

Once, Tommy and his younger brother Chris and I found a bloated pig washed up. Its greenish skin and fly-eaten head warned us of whatever ooze had pumped up its ripe mass to obscenity. Though we three pirates sharpened a spear, we dared not burst its ballooning belly. We trudged far upwind of the thing and roasted wieners and marshmallows on a "box" fire assembled according to instructions in *Boy's Life* magazine. Afterward, we haltingly shared how much we thought we knew about sex and took comfort in our mutual ignorance. Some years later on a similar beach, I would court my high school sweetheart below the sightlines of her dutifully watchful mother.

In winter, the lake could close over me if I slipped on a snow bank or tried an unproven ice donut. Heedless of obvious danger, Skipper

Jones and Tommy and I hiked over rows of snowbanks shaped as frozen giant waves the beach had hurled back at the far open water, while the unseen tide beneath our feet slapped against them. One rare January morning, skates slung round our necks, we boys tramped over pack ice a half-mile out to a trapped pool of perfectly smooth meltwater ice, a natural hockey rink whose snow-circle edges were our boards while our boots were the goal posts. We did not heed the spidery lines in the black ice below us or that we should care where we skated.

When the last gasp of Hurricane Hazel hit us in 1954, I stood on top of the thirty-foot cliff to watch. Fierce whitecaps thrashed the bank and sprayed up over my head. The horizontal rain and violent winds could have blown me over, entombed me inside the torrent. I found out later that Hazel killed eighty-one people in Toronto alone. What I remember from that day is not being able to breathe against the wind.

The beach was also my shooting range. My father, who had never held a firearm even in wartime, bought me a Cooey .22-calibre repeater rifle and longs, shorts and mushroom dumdum ammunition. My dominant eye being left and my grip right, I positioned my chin so it touched the gunstock and waited for the bobbing stick to pass the 7x scope's crosshairs. On one occasion, Joe, my classmate and an experienced hunter of small game, took me back into the bush behind his place to shoot our rifles. In stark outline, I saw a bird gripping the side of a birch tree about ten feet off the ground. I tested my steady aim and blew it off the bark. I knew Joe would spread the word at school, and I could walk a little prouder. When we found the bird, a yellow-bellied sapsucker, its beak was grotesquely open, its eyes all but closed, its breast feathers still gently pulsing. Too stupefied to take action, I watched Joe smash its head upon a rock twice in quick succession. After that shot, I pulled back the bolt to open the breach, pointed the barrel to the ground and walked home alone. I have never pointed a gun at another living thing. To this day, I wonder if that was the reason my father gave me that rifle.

On the odd lonesome day when there were no ants to burn up with my magnifying glass, I walked the two miles to Grimsby Beach along the shore. In most places where high water swamped the beach, rock piers used for farmers' irrigation pipes presented themselves to climb over. Other places called for wading with shoes in hand, feet sinking into the slippery sand. No barrier was impassable, even if getting past it meant climbing up the bank to trespass on someone's lawn. Cliff residents thought they owned the beach, too, but I knew they didn't, at least not up to the high-water line, no matter how much they had paid to keep the lake at bay.

With casting and fly reels, and any gear we could muster, we boys fished for perch off the farmer's pier and usually came up with sunfish or rock bass too small and bony to bother with. Sometimes, an overwrought cast resulted in a horrendously tangled backlash that would sideline one of us for hours while the others kept fishing and offered no help picking apart the loops of line. During the spring smelt run, we watched men dip big square nets, like inverted dome tents, into the black water at night by the light of fires set to attract the fish. When they hauled them up, some would hold a bushel's worth of writhing fish in them. After we went home, the farmer's illegal night lines trolled in the current for whitefish, trout, walleye, bass, pike, pickerel and whatever unknown monsters roamed those deeps.

In the 1950s, QEW paving excavation and local escarpment quarries gave farmers blasted stone boulders to build piers for their irrigation pumps. The eroding shoreline quickly became a scalloped rick-rack of curves and promontories below the farms. Now, homeowners cling to their lakefront with all manner of engineered contraptions to hold back the planet's strongest agent of erosion. Excess concrete poured into giant blocks may slide into the sand in two seasons. Cages of rocks cabled together to shore up a sloped incline work for a few years. Most people cannot afford the prohibitive cost of a successful interlocking steel wall. Each winter, the undercutting waves and drilled nesting tunnels of cliff swallows crack more land away from the edge. Ironically, property owners still pay taxes on the disappeared ridge.

These days I'm in my sixties; I hardly ever go down there. When I do pass a public beach access, fewer with every development the tax-hungry councils permit, I see a father and child, a couple of teens, a dog off its leash at last, some broken beer bottles in a pile of ashes and perhaps a swimmer or two daring the impure waters. I am glad my parents allowed me to grow up when I did. The terrible lake was my uncivilized refuge. In the last days of my childhood, when I was not afraid, I could fend for myself. There on the edge, where things go unnoticed and challenge awaits, I lived in a state of grace I had not earned. I had no need to "light out for the territory." The lake was my territory.

Lake Sociology

In the afternoon heat
carp colonies
snake the surface

A solitary
arrows toward me
his armour parting
the common minnows
and seeing I am not rock
he slides into the sun

Cloyed gulls scream
equivocation

In tomorrow's absences
scavenging carp
spawn in the cove
the shad nation
rattles its bones
swallows drive
me inland

The Scapegoat

I was seven when I learned that confession can be good for much more than the soul.

The story goes like this:

Mrs. Queenie Brown, the Headmistress of Knewnham College Preparatory School, and our class's teacher, believed in corporal punishment for non-capital offences. The receiving positions were two: either you bent over and offered your behind, or you held out your hand … And if you flinched or pulled your hand back or curled your fingers in anticipation, you would receive a follow-up swipe harder than the first, and beyond what the sentence required, though what that number was, we were never told. It likely depended upon how many strokes it took to raise the blood and turn the skin pink. To be fair, no blood was ever drawn, and nothing more than a stinging palm could be exhibited to classmates as one's own red badge of courage. For serious offences, then, a stinger to the hand; for spelling mistakes and the like, the behind. That was "teaching to the test" in 1952. I became a good speller and rarely had to submit to the cane, a bamboo switch about one-quarter inch in diameter, with a curved handle for better grip.

The cane was a staple of British education, a final arbiter of power. So it was all the more serious when this cane went missing. A disarmed and red-faced Mrs. Brown threatened to keep the entire class after school if the thief didn't confess and return it. Minute after minute as we sat stiff and silent, hands clasped on our desks, backs straight as boards – bad posture being another caning offence, after dirty fingernails and dropping h's and g's from beginnings and endings of words – certain consequences began to form in my mind.

My travel to and from school was by the Number 10 bus, which stopped down the street and around the corner from the school's entrance. I was now deemed grown up enough to ride the bus by myself. My bus home arrived about 4:30 p.m. each day, summer or winter. In early December, at 4:30 on a school day approaching the shortest day of the year, darkness was in the offing. And on this day, so was rain. If I missed the bus, which now seemed very possible, I would have to find my way home on foot, in the dark and the rain, through streets lit only by the occasional orange street lamps. I would be shivering with the penetrating damp cold. I may become lost. Alone on the streets of Illford, without shelter or company, I might wander about all night long, afraid to close my eyes for the danger lurking in every shadow. I might come to harm.

The culprit was evidently bent on keeping mum about the theft. Tension gathered in the room. The standoff seemed unresolvable. Fear triggered my adrenalin.

It occurred to me that although I did not do it, perhaps I could confess anyway.

If I confessed to stealing the cane, I might not only free myself from imprisonment but also free the rest of the class. My grand self-sacrifice would make me a hero of the Christ ("Greater love hath no man …") or Sydney Carton ("'Tis a far, far better thing that I do …") calibre. Of course, at seven years old, I had not understood either of these heroes, but I sensed that opportunities for easy heroism didn't come every day. I could take away the sin of the school, free our unidentified Barabbas from certain punishment and save my mates in the bargain.

Slowly, I stood up.

Were they shocked that I, the least likely to offend, had done this deed? Now that the burden of collective guilt had been lifted from them, many were relieved and instantly became curious onlookers to the next phase of this drama. Ironically, no one wanted to leave.

"Haskins, my office. The rest of you are dismissed."

My punishment was to be too horrible for the class to witness. The door of escape closed behind me.

Perhaps Mrs. Brown had realized her position was untenable. Perhaps she was glad to have been delivered a way out. At any rate, I remember being scolded, though it seemed her heart wasn't in it. Most importantly, I remember not being hit. My parents would have to be informed, of course. They never were. I was excused in time to catch my bus.

The spoils of lying didn't last long. Children have short memories. Other daily events took precedence, and I slipped quietly back down the ladder of notoriety to what had become my comfort zone. Things hadn't worked out as I had foreseen. I didn't much like the temporary spotlight. It shone too brightly on my shortcomings.

A few days later, another cane appeared, similar to the first. It was suspended from a nail next to the blackboard in full view of all of us. The reins of power had not shifted. Strangely, this cane was never taken down from its perch.

A Child's Christmas in Beamsville

Childhood memories drift together like wood smoke from neighbour-hood chimneys, each fireplace a sun of its own galaxy of rosy-cheeked children and red-nosed uncles, fussing aunts and the faithful dog who settles far enough away from any commotion not to get stepped on but close enough to still bask in the warmth of the flames.

Our Christmas always began on Christmas Eve at Midnight Mass. While the last parishioners filed in before the service and found their places standing down the side aisles and along the back, I would sing "O Holy Night" solo from the front choir stall, with only Mrs. Orval Smith at the organ for company. My starched ruffled collar scratched my neck, my tie threatened to choke off my treble voice, my face and ears flushed with nervous heat. As the entire congregation watched me, all I could think about was that last high G on "di-*vine*" and whether it would come out uncracked at that late hour. Would I have the confidence to think above the note and land solidly on it? Would I fear it and crack into silence? Or would I opt out and go for the lower third, knowing that everyone in the congregation had been waiting for the climactic high crescendo? And then, as if by some heavenly ordination, the note came out strong and pure, and my mother, who sang alto, sighed, and my father, who sang bass and led the choir, released his white-knuckled grip on the hymnal. With each passing year, this annual ritual of courage and stamina became riskier as my voice approached the breaking stage, after which I would never again sing in public.

The ordeal over, I was soon nodding off during the sermon, and again after the Kyrie and the Communion hymn, "O Come, All Ye Faithful," which never lasted beyond the fourth row of communicants coming to the rail. Once again, I hoped that this Christmas

Eve the snow would be softly falling outside our candle-lit sanctuary. Then we would recess out of the church to the peal of the steeple bell, rung double time by Mr. Earle, the Warden, who was sufficiently rotund not to leave the floor with each upward yank of the rope. We choirboys sloshed into a Christmas morning snowfall wet enough for perfect snowballs. Beneath a sky now peppered with stars, among them the one star that must still hover over Bethlehem and us, we packed ice-balls and pelted each other, half-heartedly missing the dawdling parishioners, but not their cars, never their cars. As our black cassocks trailed in the slush and our white surplices darkened with direct hits, we began to drift back to our parents and our homes, and to the chance of opening one present before bed – one small present to quell the excitement and perhaps grant our parents a reasonable waking when daylight came, though the peace never lasted past the moment our eyes opened to greet Christmas Day.

Canada being the country of the North Pole, Father Christmas came to my house first, while his sack was still full. My English friends would have to wait their turn. And though our two chimneys were sealed shut and the pitch of our roof was as steep as the church's, he did come. While we slept, he loaded the tree with presents tagged in my mother's handwriting, and we never questioned why only one present, always the biggest, was from our parents while he had brought so many.

One Christmas, when I was ten, I sinned. I sinned against the understood conventions of Christmas. I discovered an HO-gauge electric train set, with the orange diesel engine, stuffed underneath my parents' bed. It would replace the Hornby train I had to leave behind in England when we emigrated. Once again, I could wear my Hornby Engineers button in my lapel and be part of the imaginary club of little engineers I had also left behind when we embarked on our voyage for Beamsville in 1953. Canada, where there were grizzlies and lumber-jacks and red-coated Mounties like Sergeant King, whose adventures I had listened to on the BBC, and even wild Indians. Perhaps because it was Christmas, my knowing parents never confronted me with my crime, not of finding the train but of looking for it.

When the wrapping paper had been carefully removed and folded and put away for next year, and the train tracks, in a figure eight with a side spur to a rotary turntable, covered the living room floor, and the cats, having exhausted their curiosity with the lighted locomotive, were asleep on the arms of the couch like bookends, we sat down to dinner. All the smells from the kitchen swam to the dining room table set with crystal from my rich Uncle George's fine china and glassware shop in Philadelphia. Mum lit the candles. Dad sharpened the carving knife with a flourish of expert strokes of the round file, honing each side of the blade to the acid test of sharpness. If the file proved too coarse to give the razor edge he sought, out would come the whetstone, and the ritual would continue into its second phase. Only when he rolled up his sleeve and shaved the hair off the back of his wrist was he satisfied that the knife was ready to carve. Finally, he would skewer the beast and slice the thinnest slivers off the roast.

"The meat fairly falls apart, my dear," he would say, knowing this would put a modest smile on my mother's face as she dealt out the roasted potatoes and peas and carrots and the richest mushroom gravy in the world.

After my sister and I cleared away the dinner plates, my mother produced the desserts — never one but several: apple pie and sour cherry pie with ice cream, mince pies, raspberry swirl dotted with coloured marshmallows, trifle covered in meringue and Christmas pudding dusted with icing sugar and topped with a sprig of real red-berried holly from the garden. We sampled each one until our bellies threatened to burst. And then out came the sherry and the port, and my sister and I, the bobby-soxer and the whippersnapper, were permitted a small glass to mark the extraordinary import of the occasion.

The dog cleaned up the scraps, we kids washed the dishes and our parents retired to the living room to hear the young Queen's

Christmas message replayed. I mittened up for an afternoon in the snow, trying out the new toboggan in the middle of the road or rolling heavy balls of snow for the droopy snowman who would guard our front door for as long as the cold snap held. Soon I would meet the Whitelaw boys, and we'd walk up to the brickyard pond for a game of hockey and a chance to wield my new "Rocket" hockey stick like Maurice Richard. We got Tommy, who had a severe underbite, to clear the ice with the yellow warning sign that always fell down in the first freeze-up, because we wanted to hear him say "Trethpathers will be Perthecuted." A rather grubby boy whose name we didn't know, but who had perfect teeth and who always forgot his skates, volunteered to play goal. We let him, because although the rule was "no lifting," Jim Hildreth was playing today, and Jim had joined a real team in town and knew how to sweep the puck out of reach around the defender's blind side and swoop in for the goal shot, which didn't always stay along the ice.

As the sun went down behind the bulldozed clay mounds, we sat around on the snowbanks puffing on Old Port cigarillos and watched the pretty figure skaters watching us blow smoke rings. Except for little Anna, who took umbrage at one of us for no apparent reason and yelled across the pond in our general direction, "You dirty skunk!" and stomped off.

When we got back home, our fingers were numb with cold and all but shattered, we feared, like that North Pole explorer I had read about in *Boy's Annual*, whose toes froze black and broke off and crumbled away in his hands. Then gangrene set in and they had to amputate his feet with only a large Bowie knife and a half-bottle of whisky for anesthetic. Mum, not having heard that tale, held my hands under the warm tap, and then Dad rubbed the blood back into them while I grimaced. Then mugs of hot chocolate were passed around, made not with the Nestle's Quick instant powder we used after school, but with real Fry's Cocoa and brown sugar and steaming frothy milk and a single marshmallow, with a cube of Mrs. Whitelaw's homemade maple fudge on the side.

Shortly before bedtime, Dad pulled down a tiny copy of *A Child's Christmas in Wales*, and we tried to listen to him read to us while we watched the new coloured electric candles on the tree bubble up and down. When he got to the part about "Mr. Daniel looks like a spaniel," my sister went off in a fit of giggles, and then we all started in, and then my father pretended to get annoyed and threatened that next year it would be *A Christmas Carol* and that was much, much longer.

There were to be many other Christmases in the coming years, when a chosen dear one sat with us at table and hearth, and then our own children. And if these things did not happen exactly as retold here, then still they keep Christmas alive for an old man. What is Christmas if not a feeling that all is well with the world, and that next year it will come again to children and grandchildren who will make their own memories?

Georgie C.

George C. Clifton was a small man with a quiet temperament and a clear liking for the sound of his own voice, characteristics he shared with my father. He had attained the position of principal in our country elementary school, where his unconventional ways drew unwanted attention from the Home and School parent committee and from Board officials.

Such was the state of the art in teaching methodology in 1956 that Georgie C. brought in yellow chalk to use on green boards and told us it was easier to see than white on black. He also tested us with the first Stanford-Binet IQ tests the province had provided, over much dissension from our parents. The position taken at the Home and School meeting was that each child should be given equal opportunity and attention, and should not be differentiated according to IQ scores that likely couldn't be trusted. Parents were concerned that the test disadvantaged students with low language facility or short attention spans unrelated to intelligence. He further compounded their fear of preferential treatment by calling us up to his desk in turn and quietly showing us our scores. I was pleased to clock in at 135, though I thought the number must be wrong, since no one should get more than 100 on any test. Nothing changed in the classroom after that, and the results disappeared without incident. Perhaps he was following orders, pacifying the powers that be in this one requirement so he would be left alone to carry on in his own unique way. Perhaps he was just curious to find out more about us.

Never one to let books stand in the way of education, his greatest lesson took a month of afternoons away from the curriculum. It involved the making of an Indian headdress from feathers, down, leather strips and thong, all materials as authentic as we could gather. My job was to bring in the white down from chickens to be wrapped around the base of whatever Georgie C. was able to procure that would stand in for eagle feathers. I went to Peter Thompstone's house, a tall Victorian Gothic farm home on the escarpment bench, when his father and mother were wringing the necks of chickens – I had so hoped to see one running about with its head cut off – and plucking them on their back porch. I gathered up the tiny feathers by the bagful, careful to leave behind the bloodstained ones and to get away from there before I was roped into helping out, a horrifying prospect.

Next day in class, each of us was given one long brown feather to wrap. Mysteriously, we began to learn how patience and skill and care for this artifact could generate respect for the people we now call our First Nations. Four years earlier in an English schoolyard, I had played Cowboys and Indians – never having met either, of course. I learned to die with such flair when shot that I got to be an Indian most often, though of course every histrionic dying lasted much longer than the death that followed it. For sixty years, however, I have carried Georgie C.'s interest in Indians of the coast, plains and forest and consider this lesson to be the most valuable of all my childhood teachings.

In the wood shop, he showed those of us who had never lifted a hammer how to use hand tools, the difference between a crosscut saw's and a ripsaw's teeth, and how to sharpen a chisel to use on hard walnut. We went home that summer proudly bearing gifts of trivets, bookends and doorstops for our parents to marvel at. I began to buy my own tools with my cherry picking money. The summer before entering high school, I built a solid workbench in our back shed out of two-by-fours and two-by-sixes, as well as two wobbly sawhorses and the box sections, or supers, of a beehive, which was to be my grade nine science project. We bought an old hive complete, so I gave the supers I had made to my father to use as cold frames for his seedlings.

Not able to resist a "teaching moment," Georgie C. also blew the snot out of his nose after working in the basement wood shop for the afternoon and showed the rag to us all so we would know what black crud our prepubescent nose hairs were hopefully screening from our lungs.

When he put official curriculum and textbooks aside and followed his own project ideas, he invoked the ire of the Superintendent of Schools, Alex Klim, a man with the wavy hair, square jaw and righteous air of a television evangelist, and an eidetic memory that amazed every child he called by name after only one encounter. Mr. Klim sat at the back of our class for the whole afternoon to inspect Georgie C. Then he spoke to us about playing fair and living a good life and believing God's word. We thought we were the ones who had been inspected. Afterwards, he gave out to each of us a maroon pocket-sized Gideon's New Testament, a ministry that his job afforded him opportunity to pursue. We buried the Testaments in our desks along with pencil sharpenings, old lunch food dried into nut-like nuggets, elastic-band slingshots with paper clip missiles, tattered workbooks, occasional mouse droppings, squashed baseball gloves, crinkled paper airplanes, and crumpled notes from classmates. We passed the notes around during memory work recitations, the easiest way to fill the hundred-line quota being A. A. Milne's rollicking "The King's Breakfast":

> The King
> asked
> the Queen
> and the Queen
> asked
> the dairymaid ...

Georgie C. imparted other life skills to us, often without intending to but with considerable flair. Wearing his suit jacket to prove his competence, he would put his finger through the loop handle on a heavy gallon glass jug full of blue-black ink, swing it up and over the crook in his arm and, by slowly lifting his elbow, pour the ink into our inkwells, whose openings were the size of a fifty-cent piece, without spilling a drop. This is how I pour cider from gallon jugs, without spilling a drop.

Or, sitting at his desk, he would watch a fly land and swoop his open hand over top of it, trapping it in his fist as it rose backward to take off. Then he would raise his fist to his ear, or to ours, and shake it to hear the frantic buzzing of wings as evidence of his success, and with a flourish of his upraised hand, hurl the hapless creature onto the floor, listening for the click of its body, the *coup de grâce*, on the tile. I, too, consider myself an expert flycatcher, though more than one glass has gone flying off the table in my enthusiasm.

As part of the compulsory entertainment portion of our monthly Red Cross meeting, I had to stand in front of the class and sing in a boy's unbroken treble voice, "O for the wings, for the wings of a dove" from Mendelssohn's anthem "Hear My Prayer," which I had rehearsed for the Kiwanis Music Festival. It was the first time I had shown my classmates that while I could not win a fight with the class bully in the washroom – for which Georgie C. admonished me, "Some boys fight with their fists, some fight with their mouths" – I could do something they could not. I sloughed off the boys' ridicule and hoped in vain that I might have impressed Diane or Josie or Nancy or any one of the unattainable lovelies, especially Helen, in our senior year.

That bully who had punched me out had a more repulsive way to garner attention. Encircled by admirers at the back of the playground, he ate worms. Again, Georgie C. reacted with peculiar restraint. "Worms probably have a good deal of protein," he quietly remarked, and that was that. After my drubbing, the boy invited me back to his house, a ramshackle hovel that explained why he wore the same clothes every day and stank, but not why the school health nurse pointedly told us all after examining his mouth that he had no tooth decay because the harmful bacteria that caused it simply didn't live in his mouth. He gave me several carpet squares as a peace offering, samples from his older brother's temporary sales job, and I took them home to line the floor of my creekside dugout fort. I never invited him to my place.

I wrote my first story for Georgie C., an account of my journey from Southampton to Montreal by ship in 1953. He liked it enough to keep it, which now I regret, as I would like to read it again, having forgotten some of the on-board hijinks my deck friend and I got up to. And yet, had he not praised it, I might never have been encouraged to take up writing in my adult life. Today, my own file drawers contain several pieces of my students' writing, decades after I taught them, and after many have become successful writers in their own fields.

One day, the boys in our grade seven/eight class picked up Georgie C.'s Volkswagen Beetle and carried it around behind the school building, out of sight. To escape detection, we all went straight home at the three o'clock bell. We never heard a word about the incident from him, but next day the car was back in its dedicated spot in the parking lot again. Oddly, he repaid our prank with various acts of kindness. He let us off cleaning the chalk brushes and boards, for example, if we washed his car.

The one most anticipated forum for academic excellence was the annual spelling bee. These were class, then school and finally county competitions. Lower Thirty, so named for being below the escarpment and thirty miles west of Niagara Falls according to some lost traveller, was a small four-room school. We had never competed in more than our own class contests until my final year. I had been a perfect speller in England by the age of seven, and yet here in Canada, I misspelled the simplest words like "aunt" or "bought" because I heard their apparent homonyms ("ant," "box") dictated in this unfamiliar Canadian accent. Yet in Georgie C.'s class, I once again excelled. I won the school competition.

On to the county bee. One night in the dead of winter, Georgie C., my parents and I piled into his VW and beetled our way through death-defying snowdrifts along unlit concessions to a small hamlet called Caistor Centre, which even today seems the centre of nowhere. Here, I was to take on the best of the county's spellers in a first-ever spell-off. A country school's pupil may meet a town school's pupils once a year at softball finals if they were exceptionally lucky, but never a city school's champions. Never in front of one's parents. Never in front of one's teacher, who had personally brought me to this remote and secret ritual. Suddenly, this wasn't to be about me. I was merely the standard bearer. It was about the class where my friends and those who were not my friends had unwittingly wagered their reputations on my performance; it was about the school for whom I was David against the Goliaths the rest of the county had mustered; it was about my parents whom for once I had the chance to make proud; and it was about Georgie C., as payback for his IQ test results, his skill with Indian head gear, his courage to follow what he felt was the right thing to do, his praise of a young boy whom he had driven to this showdown.

I do not remember the first word I was given. I know it was a monosyllable. Too easy. I rattled off the letters … and slammed on the silent *e*. The moment I said it, even before I had finished hearing myself say it, I knew I had brought crashing down the whole edifice of expectations. The word had no silent *e*. I managed to shuffle off the stage into the audience to sit between my mother and Georgie C., where in silence I endured shame on a biblical scale, the shame of a schoolboy's hubris, not daring to wipe the tears from my face lest I make even more public my disgrace. On the car ride home, nothing was said but my father's merciful pontificating about gardening matters, so I did not have to speak. Nothing was ever said.

When I was hospitalized for an extremely painful operation, Georgie C. had the class draw and paint cards wishing me well and brought them to my bedside. He also came to our house during my recuperation to bring me homework and to visit with me and my parents. My father and he swapped scouting stories, as both had been active in the movement. The next year, when we bought an old house in town, we found out that he, a bachelor, lived like a hermit in an upstairs room in a boarding house across the road from us, and we hardly ever saw him. Soon after that, he was gone.

Some years later, when I had become a teacher, the inspector who had given out the New Testaments told me that Georgie C. had burned to death in a cabin fire in the bush in northern Ontario. I used the ending of his life in a story about a fictional character I had to bump off, a story I submitted to a national CBC story competition. My entry won over nine hundred others.

Enough

The bulb had been changed. My room was once again dimly bathed in the minimal light cast by a single, bare 40-watt bulb positioned dead centre in the ceiling. In one corner, a shaky card table served as a desk. Wherever I sat, the book was in my shadow. If I slumped in bed to read, the pages were darkened by their own tilt away from the bulb. The landlady must have changed it during my Saturday morning lecture – rocks and stars, Geology and Astronomy for artsies – and at what peril to her five-foot-two-inch Anglo-Saxon frame god knows. Had she teetered atop some circus apparatus of chair parts, risking her life for pennies saved by reducing the wattage from the 100-watt bulb I had installed in a venture of secrecy and defiance? Or perhaps she had coerced my neighbour in the adjoining room, a hefty frosh footballer named Chuck who figured out that an introduction to tertiary education meant a good prospect of getting laid the first week or, failing that, of being so pissed drunk on campus booze that any objective other than remaining conscious was pointless. In any case, I had to deal with the humiliation not only of being discovered but of being trumped. The 100-watt bulb had been confiscated; it was to be 40 watts or darkness.

Mrs. Berwick – she had Americanized *berrick* into *burr-wick*, interestingly crossing a weed with a candle – had two calls. "Oh boyeez" meant we were in for some hot chocolate, made from scratch in a saucepan with real milk, cocoa and sugar while we watched. We would have shovelled the snow for a week to earn this reward. "Daayve," meant I was in for another scolding, for being late with the $14 weekly rent, or for failing to scrub down the shower stall and replace the floor mat on the towel bar, or, today, for changing a light bulb. I did not wish to lie about something as meagre as a bulb's wattage, the way Algernon had lied about eating Lady Bracknell's cucumber sandwiches in Oscar Wilde's play *The Importance of Being Ernest*. We literary undergrads had heard of the kerfuffle a cucumber sandwich could cause, so I did not take the current situation too lightly.

"Daayve, you must turn off the light when you leave your room. I found it on when I was cleaning. I have to be careful. If the electric bill goes up, I'll have to increase my rents. Living alone isn't easy at my age, you know ..."

She didn't look at me, but stared at the saucepan whose brown contents she was steadily stirring. Not a word about switching bulbs. No admission on her part, no accusation of what I had done. A simple cup of hot cocoa as an apologetic compromise, an assumption of mutual understanding. Then we could both carry on as landlady and tenant, returning to our separate floors – she secure in her victory, and I determined to bring back a desk lamp from home at Christmas.

Things abated after that. Soon I was falling behind in my studies, particularly history, which I would forego in favour of extra philosophy classes with George Grant or John Thomas, the former promulgating the notion that Aristotle might as well have been a Christian and the latter being the father of rock star Ian and comic hoser Dave, and both therefore well worth my attention. There were bright spots, like the time the entire undergraduate class brought tape-recorders to tape Dr. Berners W. Jackson's pre-taped Shakespeare lectures, leaving the room empty but for thirty machines busily learning from one, as the story goes. Or the time I myself spied Dr. Jackson in his ubiquitous gown at the corner convenience store in downtown Westdale rifling through an upper-shelf copy of *Gent*, only to see him produce the same copy as evidence at a later seminar on Censorship in Presbyterian Ontario. Turns out the son of Hamilton Mayor Lloyd D. Jackson was on the Ontario Board of Censors at the time and tempered his Shakespearian scholarship with a dollop of trollops in snuff films and the quest for redeeming social values in films like *I Am Curious Yellow* and *Last Tango in Paris*.

I digress.

The whole thing came to a head one night in early November, after the in-class return of a failing history paper and the posting of the December exam schedule. I re-evaluated my options: cut my losses and let the Saracens and Crusaders fight it out without me, or sink ever deeper in the encyclopedic morass of names, dates and facts that constituted Medieval History. I hate history. I can't remember dates. Charlemagne invented the horse. Robin Hood invented the longbow. I remember that stuff. I had failed only one exam in high school, and that was Christmas exam in Grade Ten History. Now I was going to flunk my first semester at university. I was going to the Dean's Tea Party for sure, the one where he tells me I'm not suited for university life and I'm going home to my immigrant parents who had scrimped and saved their way to respectable poverty to send me here.

I lay down on my cot – I could not dignify it by calling it a bed – beneath the 40-watt bulb and began to shiver. I wasn't cold. My muscles were seizing up, my body convulsing into panic mode, my eyes tearing. I had the DT's without the alcoholic catalyst. For the first time in my life, I was out of control – entirely, inescapably, helplessly. I shook through minutes, then hours deep into the night, as the realization that this might never stop during my lifetime began to suggest Hemingway's option, *Death in the Afternoon*, or rather the wee hours. Death came in true Shakespearean fashion, in the form of sleep from exhaustion, my body and brain simply giving up, refusing to participate any longer as the new sun washed my eyelids with orange and released me to a merciful, dreamless slumber.

There was to be no revelation. I simply woke up. I think it was to the sound of "Daayve" curling up the staircase to my door.

I never brought the desk lamp from home. I moved the cot to the wall and the table underneath the light fixture. I made do. That's what we Brits do. It's what got us through the war. It would get me through this bloody backlog of work, under this bloody bulb that had lit my room on the one night of my life when, under the weight of the world – albeit the medieval world – I collapsed in debilitating despair to which I would never again surrender. Just a 40-watt bulb, but it was enough.

Tables in a University Cafeteria

Remember
in the wintertime
        we got so far
behind

Hands

        I improvised

                and then the kids come home
       went to paint
plant a yellow geranium
       in
the air   trigonometry?   the eavestrough
       Phenomenal!

The geranium fingers
       the essence of it
traffic in a
      really basic

              yellow stain
glass ant house
         I got so pissed off
             I don't drink coffee
       doing a whole section
       and saying
    maybe that's good
      "what's wrong?"

41

In the underworld
       went to New York city
blue snakes
       gonna take Indian music
caress a sterile
            well it's incredible
                   they mess it up so bad
          I lost thirty cents
               it's not worth doing
          in that fucking thing
chair
      maybe that's good

                 I really don't know
     can't remember

Section Two

How to Write a Canadian Poem

Say you are from some bay or cove or tickle,
but live in Toronto.
Say you read Dylan Thomas,
but don't. Read Dylan.

Talk of fireflies, blackflies, bones, stones, water, mirrors,
Talk of poison ivy and first love in the same breath.
Call something a "palimpsest" and acknowledge Earle Birney.
Title it "Bushed" and acknowledge every poet before you.

Put in something to kill:
a moose in the headlights, a bear, salmon, cod,
a car, a culture, the planet, god.
Don't kill it till after it stares you down.
Don't look for history where there is none;
Look for history in trees.

Write in chopped
up prose, minus explanation.
Call your poems totems, minus punctuation.
Make "you" the poet, the reader, a lover,
and no one in particular.
Claim a hundred words for snow,
but call it snow.

Dogs, Dreams and Mercy

In my grade ten Agricultural Science class in Beamsville High School in 1958, each boy was to kill a chicken either by puncturing its brain or chopping off its head. The stigma of not manning up to this task on site would be unbearable for me, so I contracted a convenient cold and stayed home. I should have known then that I would never become what I had wanted to be all of my life: a veterinary surgeon.

I loved dogs. I never shouted orders to them. I talked to them as to a person, a child, and they responded with sympathetic understanding, if only to my tone of voice and body language. I knew to present an open hand, palm up, under the chin so as not to block their vision if I reached to stroke the head. I knew how to train obedience, build trust and earn loyalty. I never teased a dog or used it as a toy for human amusement. I could connect with a dog more easily than with a person. I enjoyed their friendliness and their devotion. In my naïveté, I thought that spending my working life healing them would be a perfect fit. Nothing prepared me for what confronted me one Sunday afternoon two years later in Guelph.

My family was attending Open House weekend at OAC (Ontario Agricultural College) on the invitation of my sister's friend. Having no wish to sample tarts with a bunch of apprentice dietitians, I seized the opportunity to investigate the veterinary college across the road. The oldest vet college in Canada had more the air of an aging gothic mansion than a welcoming hospice. English ivy climbed its walls. A central-balustrade staircase led to wide double entrance doors. A tall white cupola topped the three-storey facade. Rows of windows suggested a hundred rooms I wanted to explore.

I slipped in through an unlocked side door and was met by a waft of formaldehyde that nearly choked me. Its pungent odour assaulted my nasal passages and irritated my throat and eyes. Taking shallower breaths through the mouth helped a little. Today, formaldehyde is considered a human carcinogen and is watered down in fume hoods by someone wearing protective gloves and equipment. In the 1950s, every medical student simply got used to it.

I wandered the deserted corridors, past empty post-mortem rooms and physiology labs. I stopped to peruse a gruesome collection of samples from internal organs preserved in glass jars. Most looked like pieces of meat that were once a liver, a heart, a kidney, a lung, taken for teaching or diagnostic purposes. A whole brain about the size of an orange hung suspended in one jar. Farther down a long hall were the operating stations. All doors were closed but one, through which I heard voices. Inside, a large red setter lay anaesthetized on a gleaming metal operating table, its tongue flopping out of its mouth, its belly cut open. I could see two men in scrubs leaning over it, their hands working in the bluish-red pulp of its guts. It didn't occur to me at the time that the dog may have been a cadaver undergoing an autopsy or an organ retrieval procedure. What preoccupied me was that those hands would one day be mine.

I've heard that medical students experiencing what lies beneath the skin for the first time are filled with wondrous amazement at the complexity of the functioning parts of the body. I, however, felt a rush of nausea at the spectacle before me. In that moment, all my years of loving animals and believing that I shared a special kinship with some of them dissipated. I knew this was a place I did not want to be in, the training ground of a profession I was not suited to pursue.

That setter was the third of three dogs I shall never forget.

The first was a bedraggled mongrel I met in Quito on my way to the Galapagos Islands in 2008. Head down as though submitting to her fate, she wandered out of a small groceria beneath the disapproving gaze of the shopkeeper, ambled across the single-lane cobblestone road, curled up against the curb, rested her head on her front paws and closed her crusty eyes to the world. Mange had eaten away at her coat, scabbing the dry skin where the hair was already thinned or missing. Although her ribs did not show, she was obviously hanging onto life by a thread, with no apparent interest in prolonging it. Passersby, even children, barely gave her a glance, as though she were an untouchable, unclean and perhaps diseased. To an approaching car, she must have looked like a sack of discarded refuse hardly warranting evasive action.

The sinking sun slowly cast a shadow over where she lay. Perhaps if she escaped injury, the slight cooling might revive her enough to send her on her way to join the other night prowlers in this city of strays, at least a third of which limped from being struck by impatient drivers. Patience was about all this dog had left, and it would not likely be enough.

The second was a dog that adopted us in Essex, UK, in 1948. My clearest memory of Bobby – part border collie, part Heinz 57 – was of him slinking around the corner of our house whenever the camera came out. Only his disappearing tail was ever caught on film. A fugitive, he never wanted any photos to spoil his anonymity in the world. He had walked up from London, following the troops returning to their homes after the war, and landed on our doorstep half-starved, exhausted and near death. In those days, caring for strangers was not uncommon, so we took him in, nourished him and brought him back from purgatory. Our own family pet, a pedigreed cocker spaniel pretentiously named Silver Flash on his papers but christened Spiv by us, kept to the regular routines of a domestic pet's life. Bobby, however, was far too independent of spirit to be so tamed. His home was southern England, not our small corner. Once revived and healthy, he would wander off again to parts unknown, often for months at a time, before dragging his dishevelled, weakened body back to our hospice for renewal. He answered to the name only if it was in his interest to do so. We called him Bobby because not even the police could catch him.

Three dogs: the vagrant mongrel in the gutter in Quito, the wartime stray up from London and the red setter on the operating table in Guelph. As Arthur Miller said of Marilyn Monroe, "All she needed was a little luck to survive in this world."

Teachers

Gene is a Mohawk Indian of the Turtle Clan.
Timmy is Gene's white son.
Gene made my nephew David a club from a root
wrapped round an India rubber ball
and a necklace from an arrowhead
picked out of the dirt on his farm.
Back home in Yorkshire, David
hung up his cowboy guns.

So one evening a week
I teach Timmy to read
"opportunity class" textbooks.
Gene will make me a picture in copper to pay me
If I bring him a likeness he can copy.
I never have.

It's been a month since I've seen Timmy
My car has a cracked block
I can't get to school to pick him up.
Gene phoned
"Would you like to buy a picture?"
He's moving his family to Florida
as soon as his bills are paid.
"How much?" "Not much.
Hundred dollars. One of the big ones."
"Yeah. Well listen. I'd like to help you out
but I can't right now.

My car's got a cracked block
so we're looking to buy another
a wreck, nothing fancy
but we can't right now. We're strapped.
Matter of fact we were going to New York
on March break to see friends
an artist, lives in Manhattan
but that's out too.
About Timmy. If you can get him down here ..."

Gene phoned back
said he's got this record
of Chief Dan George with the Centennial Speech
he bought it for the Centennial Speech
and the Indian prayer and some white man's songs
and would I like to hear it.

First I thought he was going to sell it, but then
what's the price of a record
so I said Yes, I would like to hear it
and he said he'd send it with Timmy in twenty minutes
and I could send it back after his next lesson.

Timmy says in Florida he'll be doing grade nine work
his reading's coming along so well.

Nice Places to Visit

The letter arrived on one of those grey December mornings on the edge of winter when the north wind off Lake Ontario cuts through your clothing and stops you cold. Walking up the long lane through skeletal peach orchards to the mailbox, I prepared myself for another publisher's rejection, my daily dose of raised hopes dashed.

The letter I found was one of those blue folded airmails that you had to figure out which side to slit open without tearing the inside text in two. The postmark read Athens 11-11-1971. I had family in England, not in Athens. This letter had to be from Mirdza, a high school student I had taught in my first year of teaching six years ago, now graduated from McGill University and apparently living with someone she had met in Greece. My guess was correct. She wrote of her partner's recent travels in Black Africa, of the free delivery of their baby in an Athens hospital and of the police having opened their last four letters from Canada. Then, in a postscript, she had written, "Can you come to see us?"

I wondered what she was not telling me. It could have been a thinly disguised plea for help. She might have become desperately lonely. She might have wanted to see a familiar face from home, one that knew her family and spoke English. It could have been something one blurts out to seem affable, never imagining the invitation would be accepted, but not in a postscript.

My wife and I, both teachers in our twenties, had talked about doing the European circuit. This letter would tip the scales, adding Greece to the itinerary. Classical antiquity, heroes and gods. Free lodging at a midway point. I wrote back the next day, "Yes, we'll come."

An exceptionally bright English student from a Latvian working class family, Mirdza had come to see me once after high school, the day before she was to leave her home in St. Catharines to begin her undergraduate studies at McGill. On the beach below our house by the lake, we chatted about Conrad's *Heart of Darkness*, which she said she reread during the summer months. Marlow's quest into the madness that was colonized Africa enchanted her.

Mirdza was somewhat of a loner, conscientious, intelligent, independent. Her horizons were far from the family home on Cumming Street in west St. Catharines. She determined that education would help her make her mark. We talked about her heroic attempt to speak to the assembled student body when she ran for student council president. She stood on stage in a white blouse and conservative skirt and spoke into the microphone as though she were discussing politics with a friend. The sound didn't carry. She was received with polite applause, then lost hands-down to the boy who tore up his speech, if in fact it was his stump speech, and swallowed a goldfish instead. She didn't mind losing, she said, because she had put her argument down on paper and gone public with it. That was what mattered to her. As for the rest, well, people get what they deserve.

After that visit, I did not see or hear from her for four years.

Then, intermittent correspondence from several countries began to arrive, most notably from the C. G. Jung Institute in Zurich, where she continued her studies. These letters gave me a kind of vicarious pleasure of chatting with someone whose life was nothing like mine but whose choices were ones I might have made had my circumstances been different. A husband after six years of courting my high school sweetheart, I was doing what I was supposed to be doing. She was doing what she wanted to be doing, I thought.

Perhaps I saw something of myself in her. My best experiences as a student were at university. As much as I had wanted to start my life as an adult, I soon missed the challenge of collegial thinking and wished I'd stayed on for grad school.

For Mirdza, the bloom fell off the rose. The exciting year of study in Europe began to look like a life there, far from the home she had wanted to leave. She felt isolated, first in Switzerland and then in Athens, where she picked up some freelance writing, hardly the breakout career. The simple tasks of daily living tired her. Doing laundry required negotiating time with the washing machine in a foreign language without unintentionally offending someone's sensitivities. Every day, she had to make new acquaintances, knowing these people would not become friends. Too much effort for too little forward progress, always with the worry of earning enough money to keep going.

And finally, this invitation. Not much to pack up and go halfway around the world on, with my wife, Bev, and her long-time friend, Anna, in tow. As for myself, London, Paris, Rome were all a scenic diversion from Athens. On the final night on board the oversold ferry from Brindisi to Patras, we three together on pilfered couch cushions squeezed together on the crowded deck. When the alternative is cold floorboards to sleep on, you guard your bed with the same vigilance that you protect your passport, and you avoid eye contact with those opportunistic predators who were your fellow adventurers a few hours ago.

∾

We disembarked and bused into the city. The expressway into Athens was lined with billboards of American oil companies – Mobil, Esso, Texaco – tinged orange in the late afternoon sun, a peculiar welcome to tourists seeking antiquity, and the only familiar signage we would see. Street names in the Greek alphabet bore no resemblance to those on our city map. To find our way, we would have to rely on the kindness of taxi drivers, who also spoke in their own language, of course.

Trial and error eventually landed us near Mirdza's door on Trapezountos, a residential crescent in a neighborhood characterized by five-storey apartment blocks. Bent over with luggage, I walked behind the girls up the slight incline to Mirdza's building, hoping I would not be puffing too hard when we finally faced each other.

I buzzed the fourth-floor apartment. "I'll come down," she said through the crackling speaker. It was the first time I'd heard her voice in years. The elevator, about the size of a water closet, with a hand-operated iron-grill safety gate, ground to a stop with a final shudder like a dog shedding water after a swim. She emerged, looking as if we'd interrupted her doing dishes or feeding the baby. We shared greetings without touching in the narrow foyer. She seemed anxious to take advantage of the elevator before someone else diverted it.

"We can't all get in at once. Why don't you two go on up, and Dave and I will follow you. You have to pull the door shut after you're inside and open it when it stops. We're number three. Hank will be at the door."

Bev and Anna disappeared somewhat nervously into the elevator, leaving me alone with Mirdza. For a moment, we smiled at each other in a "mission accomplished" sort of way, and I saw again the endearing dimples at the corners of her mouth. She was as I remembered her, young and sparkling.

We chatted comfortably, more like neighbors than world travelers.

"How was the ride?" she asked.

"Fine. We had to get two taxis. The first one never heard of Trapezountos."

"Oh, you have to tell them 'Gouthi' and then stop them when you see our street. You say '*ndaksi*.' It means 'OK, stop, this is fine' – pretty much anything you want. They'll let you out at the corner and you can walk up the hill."

"'Daxi,' right. Where's Gouthi?"

The elevator shivered and groaned against our weight, and my oversized suitcase squeezed between us. There was more talk of how cheap the taxis were. Then, Hank at the grill, suddenly comic in undershorts and slippers. He was shorter than I'd expected. I thought his practised smile and closely cropped hair that never needs attention must serve him well on his business trips, but from Mirdza's letters describing his work in Africa and the Middle East for his Dutch employer, Elsevier Publishing, I had imagined a more commanding presence. I couldn't see him in a suit and tie.

We managed a perfunctory handshake that left the suitcases tottering and quickly stepped single file down the hall to their apartment. His easy manner, his refusal to put on any show for us at all, kept me guessing. I wondered if we were to be Mirdza's guests while he went about his business, since she had been the one to invite us.

Their apartment was modest, bright with white walls and, as it turned out, hot as blazes in the siesta hours from noon to two when the city shut down. Books and jazz records from the fifties filled makeshift shelves and boxes. A batik picturing an African woman hung from the ceiling, and an ebony "people tree" stood in one corner, artifacts from Hank's travels. Bev and I slept on ticks on the living room floor while Anna was given the second bedroom. The baby stayed with her parents and Bismarck, the dachshund.

Next morning, Hank made coffee in the galley kitchen. Beans were mixed, measured and ground, chicory and a pinch of salt added, water boiled in a green metal jug, and the coffee drip-brewed by hand pour – an affordable ritual.

Mirdza came into the room with Melissa over her shoulder. She sat opposite me and adjusted her gown to nurse. For the first time, I noticed her wedding ring.

"You've been keeping things from me," I said.

She saw me looking at her hand. She held it up to show us the gold band.

"Hank bought me this so the neighbours wouldn't talk. We'd be evicted if they found out we weren't married. They still arrange marriages here, you know, in the country. It's not as bad as it used to be, but these people don't change."

"Ignorant peasants," Hank interrupted. "Can't read or write. If you gave them the vote tomorrow, they wouldn't know what to do with it. All this noise about military dictatorship, it's true alright, but they don't care. That woman, film star, what's her name?"

"Melina Mercouri," Mirdza said.

"Zorba the Greek," said Bev. Anna looked up from her Frommer's guide.

"No, that was Irene Papas," Mirdza corrected.

"Mercouri, yeah, the one who's always making speeches in America about how oppressed the Greeks are. Well, America doesn't know this, but these people hate her. She left them. If she were to fly into Athens airport tomorrow, they'd stone her if they could. She'd get off a couple of press releases and then they'd lock her away, and nobody would give a damn. That's the way they are. You don't hear anyone talking politics in this country. You never know the person you are talking to."

He reached back for the coffee pot and sent it around the table. He was on a roll.

"Listen, Greece has been threatened by everybody on her borders and occupied by most, if not territorially, then economically. The communists want to take over their government, the Americans want to park the Sixth Fleet on their shores to watch the Middle East, and the Germans won't let them into the Common Market so they can sell their fruit. The Greeks know the country belongs to everybody but them if they stop to think about it. So they don't think. They do their job, they siesta, they play backgammon all night at the corner bar. And the colonels do all the rest."

Anna, Bev and I weren't politically astute people, but when you travel, it's as well to know what's going on around you. Back in the summer of 1968, Bev and I were holidaying in Yorkshire with my sister's family when Russian tanks rolled down the streets of Prague. Everyone was glued to their TV sets, trying to assess the consequences of the crackdown. Anything can happen, any time, even in Canada. The FLQ taught us that in 1970. Now, sitting across from Bev, I think she was quietly taking in Hank's stories about the erosion of freedom in this homeland of democracy with some trepidation. The tension playing out in the country at large set the stage for the dynamics that would unfold in our little group of foreigners.

"Is that why you quit the newspaper?" I asked, turning to Mirdza.

"No. The baby made that decision for me. As for the paper, we've been lucky so far," she said. "*The Athens News* is in English, so the government feels the people won't read it anyway. If they leave us alone, they can say to the rest of the world that they still have a free press. Its time will come, though. The editor, Yannis Horn, doesn't need the job. He takes the occasional potshot at the bureaucracy for the hell of it. It's a kind of sport to him. They've threatened to close it down three times already, put him under house arrest. He makes all kinds of promises, so they release him, and then in a little while he lets them have it and they come at him again."

None of our Canadian friends would discuss such matters. Just being here in this apartment stimulated my appetite for something other than what I knew back home, something less mundane.

Next day, the girls all went for a walk without me. Mirdza wanted to take advantage of Bev's camera to get some photographs of herself with the baby. In a Greek meander–patterned green dress, she looked the picture of a young mother. She put her hair up to bear the heat so that her bangs softened her face and the slim line of her neck gave her a kind of elegance. Baby Melissa, loosely wrapped in a light cloth, happily played the character actor, reacting to every new provocation around her. Hank and I each kept to ourselves in the apartment, in what seemed like normal day-to-day living.

At five o'clock, the clouds opened up on the city streets. The Greeks say it rains in threads or in ropes. This was ropes. In minutes, traffic halted and the water rushed past the tops of hubcaps. We closed all the shutters and collapsed in the damp heat of the afternoon.

That evening, Hank left for the airport to catch a night flight to Cairo. He slipped away as though he were going out to get cigarettes.

He was living a double life of sorts. As the agent for English-language publishers of books to be approved by governments in African and Middle Eastern countries, he enjoyed the expensive hotels and the anonymity of foreign cities. He liked being escorted in a limousine – courtesy of *Al Ahram*, the largest state-owned Arab newspaper in the world – from the airport to the Cairo Sheraton as a guest of the Dutch Ambassador or the Egyptian Minister of Finance.

But there were practical considerations now that he had acquired Mirdza and the baby. Flying into target cities like Beirut, getting out before the bullets flew and hoping the plane would not be hijacked was dangerous work. War-risk life insurance was damned expensive, and his employers refused to pay for it. And if he had to insure his life, wouldn't that be admitting risk that was wrong for him as a partner and a father?

He had rescued Mirdza, possibly saved her life. He had found her sitting at an outdoor cafe in Syntagma Square, a waif at the end of her strength and her options. But living in this white oven of an apartment, sleeping with her for a month and then flying out for three more, returning the man of the world with a Moroccan pouf, he'd lost his moorings. He was spread out from Germany to Kuwait.

The day after Hank left, Bev, Anna and I toured the Acropolis. I clambered over the gleaming stones trying to frame photographs without tourists in them: the frieze on the Parthenon, the Caryatides, the distant Temple of Apollo flanked by two pillars. I stood in the cradle of democracy, on the very slope where Paul spoke to the Athenians in 51 AD. I had no idea what it all meant, but I was getting it in Ektachrome. This must be the heart of Greece. Not the quaint peasants riding donkeys through village streets, not the oil company billboards, not the heavily guarded embassies. Never mind the Instamatics, the tour buses, the pleading vendors, the multitudes with mirrored sunglasses scrambling among the ruins like insects. This hill. These stones. This defiant skyline. Our civilization began here.

That evening, Margo, a visiting roommate from Mirdza's days at McGill University, called. On Hank's suggestion, she had arranged for a friend of her Greek doctor boyfriend to take Anna out on a double date with them. Bev, Mirdza and I were alone with the music of Georges Moustaki and his balalaikas on the turntable.

"How was the Acropolis?" Mirdza asked.

"Hot. Crowded. White," I said.

"Did you go to the Plaka?"

"No. We were too tired. Maybe tomorrow."

"You should go out to Sounion. There's a daily bus that gets you there in time to watch the sun go down. It's not much of a temple, but the view out over the sea is something."

"Have you been?" I asked, hoping she would come.

"No. It's different when you live here. The city gets to you. The heat, and the monotony, it presses on you. We're not tourists or citizens. We're aliens undercover, I guess. As much as we like it here, there's always a bit of pretense involved. Like this ring."

Bismarck, their dachshund, became suddenly agitated, his nails clicking on the linoleum floor as he paced.

"Your time again?" she said to him. "I take him to a little park on a hill near here. Sometimes he meets his friends. If you would stay with Melissa?"

In the sweet relief of the evening breeze, Melissa lay asleep in their bed under the open window.

"Friends? I wonder what a Greek dog looks like."

"It's quite funny really. He was sniffing around a blue terrier one day when its owner came up and introduced himself. A Dutchman, here with some company for two years. Another day, he brought along an English girl, Margaret, and her Irish setter. So now we're a society of ex-pats."

"Will they be there tonight?"

"No. It's too late. But quite safe for a woman to walk the streets at night here. The worst that may happen is some guy following you.

They call out, but they never come close enough to touch you. It's more of a routine, something they think they're expected to do. Don't take it that I want to be alone though. I'd like some company, as a matter of fact."

Bev had been fishing in her suitcase for something. She stopped and stared at me.

"Do you want to go?" I asked.

There was a brief pause. Love wins or loses in such moments.

"You go if you like," she conceded. "I've got some letters to write."

On a small hill in the park, the dog ran loose. Mirdza and I sat on a bench, taking in the city's surprising quiet. The shadow from the path lights played up the slight hollows of her cheeks. Her eyes were uncompromising, her mouth small but full and firm. She reminded me of a picture I had of Joan Baez speaking at a peace rally. Suddenly, her voice jolted me.

"Why did you come here, Dave?"

"To the park?"

"No, to Athens. To Europe."

"Because you asked me." The answer came without hesitation.

She turned and looked off into the night.

I broke the silence. "Why did you come to Athens? What happened in Switzerland?"

She began a long story about how the courses at the Jungian Institute of Psychology had eventually bored her, how she had spent her money on train tickets to anywhere and ended up in an outdoor bar in Syntagma, drinking her last drachmas and sinking deeper into depression when Hank, dapper in an open shirt and denim suit, had literally spirited her away.

"Dave, I don't really believe how much that man loves me. I was planning how to end it when he came and took me home. I didn't even sleep with him. In this country, a girl is expected to go to bed with her date. He just said, 'Anybody can fuck.' Him, the Mediterranean stud."

"You both look like you're good for each other," I said weakly.

"Yeah, we do. About a year ago I got this need to have a child. I wanted one more than anything in the world. You know what he did? He gave me one. No strings. No wedding, no questions – he gave me a baby. Would you believe anyone could love as much as that?"

Melissa was born five weeks before we arrived.

"What about your dreams, all the things we used to write about? Have you given them up?"

"Oh no, not really. I still want to have some influence – political influence, I mean. But I've changed too. I want to contribute, but I don't see myself in the limelight anymore. I'd be content in the background, more the direction behind the leader. I don't think I'm ready for it all yet. And it doesn't matter what battleground I choose. It could be any country. Anywhere people need me."

Bismarck's tail poked up above the long grass. We let him explore. This was our time.

"I watched you roam around Europe and settle here with Hank, and I kept looking at myself, a high school English teacher, successful and stuck. You were my student, and you were on the move while I stayed behind."

I could not complete that thought to her. I could not say I wondered what my life would be like had I struck out on my own after university, as she had done.

"Anyway, I've realized that all this takes time," she continued. "I've spent my life in schools impressing others, like you in a way, and I can't even bake bread. I've only recently learned to balance a budget when Hank's away. As far as Melissa goes, we grope along from one day to the next. You see, Dave, it's good for me to stay here and keep the apartment going. I repainted the bathroom, and when Hank came home, he noticed it right away. I guess maybe that sounds trivial, but it's not. It's necessary. I need to do this for myself."

"Well, yeah, I get it. You say you need to sweep floors, but your floors are here in Athens. And your man spends six months a year plane-hopping from country to country. You asked for a child and got one. We finally gave up trying and adopted."

I thought of our two-year-old son, whom we left with my sister and her children back in Harrogate while we zipped around Europe. He was my grounding. Only because he was not here could I indulge myself on this bench with Mirdza talking into the night. My son, my wife, my job, my life. For at least this evening, Hank was not the only one leading a double life.

"You came to Europe because you wanted to," she said. "You made a start. Don't stop."

Bismarck found something in the grass to worry. She called him, and then got up and went after him. He'd be easy to lose in there. She put him on leash again but sat back down. He settled at her feet.

"You're not the first person to find our way of life attractive, you know. That surprises us. It means the less money we have, the more we are cut off from any social life, the more other people see in us what they want for themselves. We could be out of here bag and baggage when Hank's visa is up. His times away can't go on much longer, either. It's not enough, waiting for when he comes home and then living in fear of when he goes again. It's not normal."

"Hey, normal's not so great either," I said.

"His company's pressuring him," she went on. "He wants to negotiate for three months in Africa and nine months here. They say if he wants an office job, he'll have to move to head office in Amsterdam. It's a hell of a decision for him to make. He loves the sun. If it wasn't for us, he could do as he likes, be in Africa all year long if he wanted. He still might. I can't make him stay."

I couldn't think of a single reason that would make any man want to leave her.

By the time we arrived back at the apartment, Bev had turned out the sleeping bags and lay sprawled across them, rereading the letter she had written. There was no sign of Margo or Anna.

"Who did Anna go out with?" Bev asked.

"George somebody," Mirdza replied. "Dimitri knows him. And Hank's met him once or twice."

"What's he like?"

"Well, quite straight, I think. A bookseller. He stocks some propagandist stuff for the colonels, but they all do that. He's got a business to run. He doesn't want to get shut down for spreading subversion. He's a believer, though. He won't see communism, and he doesn't want democracy for another fifty years. He's made up his mind that the colonels are the best thing for now."

"No, I mean, what's he like with women?" Bev sounded anxious, almost urgent.

"Why? What happened?" Mirdza caught on.

"I'm not exactly sure. Anna came in about half an hour ago. She'd been crying. When she took off her coat, she started crying again. Seems they all four went out to supper, and then Dimitri and Margo went back to Dimitri's place. They asked Anna and George up, but George said no, and Anna figured he was being tactful, I guess. So then he ordered a taxi and they went to his place. She thought he was bringing her home. They had some sort of a scene at his door. He wanted to go to bed with her and when she refused, he started insulting her, saying what did she think they had gone out for and damning American girls for leading a man on to get his money and so on. So she ran out into the street and, luckily, got a taxi back here."

"So, old George isn't such a bookworm after all," said Mirdza. "Tell her she shouldn't let it upset her. If he paid for the meal, he paid for her, too. That's the way it is. She's lucky he didn't rape her when she refused. Hank shouldn't have set it up for them in the first place. He honestly didn't think George was up to it, though. This is the first sign of life we've seen from him."

Bev said nothing, but her look showed her shocked estrangement from this line of thinking.

"Well, I don't suppose we can do anything about it now," I said. Why did I feel I had to smooth things over?

I wondered what Anna had thought of the row. She was probably quite hurt, knowing her. Still, she wasn't so very pretty, and she was a virgin, so for George to ask her to bed, she must have felt some small particle of flattery. Anyway, she refused. She'd never know if there would have been any tenderness or not. Back in London, Ontario, there were two male prospects in her life. One was a teacher, caring, sensitive, fun-loving, who bought her skis for Christmas and planned summer holidays abroad. The other was an electrical engineer, a member in good standing of the Kitchener German Club, who bought her a colour TV for Christmas and took her house hunting in Stratford. She said no to the Greek; she was a sure bet for the German engineer.

❧

Next morning, the taxi arrived to take us to the station. Melissa was asleep upstairs. Mirdza helped the three of us, and all our paraphernalia, down to the entrance way. The driver opened the trunk for some of the suitcases, which I handed to him. Mirdza stood on the front step, mindlessly muttering about the trip and the visit and how we'd enjoy Switzerland. The trunk lid slammed down. Anna was first into the back seat, then Bev. I do not remember their goodbyes. I was on the wrong side of the car. I had to go around the front to get in the passenger side. My hand on the door handle, I turned to Mirdza. She held the front door ajar with one hand, closing the neck of her long pink robe with the other.

"Bye," I said.

Since she left St. Catharines in 1967, either she had been leaving people or people had been leaving her. "Goodbye" was too painful a word for her ever to utter.

I got into the car and the driver moved away from the curb. I knew she was waving, but I could not turn my head to see. I had not gone to her, not touched her nor kissed her. I had run away from her. I had wanted it that way. I could never touch people to show my feeling. She must have wanted it that way, too. She couldn't afford to indulge in sentiment only to face the next months alone.

My throat gagged. Tears spilled down my cheeks. I panicked a little. *No one must see this.* The driver looked only at the road. Bev and Anna, could they see? Tears rolled after more tears, running off my chin. *They'll stain my shirt. Think of the station, anything but her,* I told myself. *No, not the station: the train waits.* It wasn't working. I was weeping.

In the street outside the station, I wiped away the tears as inconspicuously as I could. They smeared my face. Bev and Anna said nothing. I was visibly guilty. Of what? Crying? Yes. For the first time since childhood.

I cried in Bev's arms.

"I can't help it," I spluttered. I was comic, pathetic. I was insulting Bev. She held me anyway.

There were four in the six-person compartment when we pulled out of Athens. I took the window seat so I could look away. Bev sat by my side, Anna opposite her and an old Greek woman in the other window seat across from me. It was hot. I could not look anywhere but outside. The land flooded past pole by pole, field by field, filling in the space between Mirdza and me. Silently, I wept on through the afternoon. Tears are motive, crime and evidence. No remorse was strong enough to stop them. I had let my handhold slip from the ledge in the first free fall of my adult life.

With the night came the mountains. The dark reflected my own image back from the window glass. The old woman wet a cloth from her water bottle and wiped off the ledge. I hadn't noticed her for hours. She took out a knife from the folds of her grey dress and began to peel an apple, placing the finished sections in a row along the ledge. The skin on her stubby fingers pulled tight, the nail edges chipped but perfectly clean. With equally deliberate motions, she devoured the apple wedges one by one. A simple routine she had likely repeated many times, one that safely anchored her in her little world. Then, she placed her hands on her lap, interlaced her fingers and remained that way for the rest of the night. She knew.

I opened the compartment door. Bodies lay in the gangway. The narrow corridor was choked with passengers sleeping on bags, leaning out of windows, huddling in bunches over a bottle of stinking ouzo. Outside on the hillsides, sentinel fires burned. Even the shepherds were watching me. I wanted to step off the train while it moved, one step down, and walk to them. I couldn't stay on this train. The train was nonsensical, evil.

Wait until Vienna. Then catch the first plane back to Athens. I can be at the apartment by tomorrow night.

The ride from Athens to Vienna took thirty-nine hours. I have never seen people treat each other with such selfish contempt. None of this mattered. Not the sweaty stink of bodies, the hot belligerence, the mad shoving for space and advantage. Not the military Yugoslav border guards taking away our passports without explanation. At twenty-eight years old, I was unexpectedly confounded by a tsunami of emotion. I had discovered that I could feel.

ↄ

After that visit, a flood of letters crossed the Atlantic; one-sided gropings for a workable perspective, delicate nuances suppressed beneath brave realizations of practicalities. None of them changed anything in the long run.

Hank resigned from his Africa posting and moved the family to Amsterdam. Melissa learned a few Dutch words at the crèche downtown. Mirdza edited scholarly manuscripts for a professor of sociology whose ambition was to establish an international forum for the world's best minds in psychology, sociology, political science and philosophy. They were always out of money, working their visas to death, and consequently eligible candidates for the housing complex of Bijlmermeer.

Bev knew that Mirdza was no threat to her, that I was the one with the problem. She thought it better to keep with what was going on than to keep apart. The summer of 1974, she agreed to leave our four-year-old son with my sister in Yorkshire again, and come to Amsterdam with me.

Bijlmermeer, Amsterdam. We saw it from the autobus a year after Athens. They lived in Klieverink, one of thirty-one concrete high-rise housing blocks with corridors a quarter-mile long, elevators every seventy yards, and a suspicion of too many people hidden away behind four hundred solid doors.

"It's a unique experiment," Mirdza explained as we sat against the living room's white walls sipping Hungarian wine. "It used to be a swamp. They drained it off and built these. The Dutch are good at reclaiming land."

From the balcony, I had seen the dry sand hills below, the browning grass and spindly saplings by the entrance ways, the motorcycle trails winding off into the distance. They were lucky. They at least had a view. Most of the tenants faced onto another concrete obstruction.

"Sociologists come out here to do surveys sometimes. There's a lot of rejects living here. Homosexuals, hookers, welfare types, a lot of blacks from Suriname – they get special immigration privileges from the Dutch colonial days. Look around the balconies at night and you'll see the red lights. Means the working girls are open for business."

One-year-old Melissa crawled out from behind the daybed and pulled herself up to standing beside the Moroccan leather pouf. Delighted with her effort, she gurgled happily. There's no more dramatic evidence of time passing than a child's growing up, witnessed in stages.

"What are the surveys for?" I asked.

"Anything from sexology to suicides. There must be fifteen or twenty thousand people out here. Probably the highest suicide rate in any concentrated area in Europe. It's insane."

"Don't believe her," Hank cut in. "These people are the same as anywhere else. It's cheap housing, that's all. What do you think happens if you put people in cement blocks in the middle of a desert?"

Just then, Felix, their Burmese cat, dashed across the reed mat and leapt up at the red African batik hanging from the ceiling. Ears pinned back, he seemed quite mad as he struggled fiercely to the top of the rippling cloth, looked sideways down and dropped.

"Jesus H Christ, keep that cat out of here!" Hank swore. Nobody moved. Felix swished his tail once and strode past him to the balcony.

"Why don't you put on some music?" Mirdza said.

"Go ahead. Clean it first. None of your muzak."

"You do it then," she said, quietly.

"Put on the Monk. And dump this while you're up." He passed up an ashtray piled with butts.

She went to a wooden box on the floor and drew out Thelonious Monk. Watching her select and clean the vinyl disc, I noticed a slight stoop in her shoulders I had not seen before.

The conversation turned to Hank, his futile attempts to find work in publishing (he had edited a few works for Elsevier, but as soon as they found out that English and not Dutch was his official second language after German, they fired him), his reading to fill the time, his new friendship with Melissa and their daily afternoon bicycle rides by the stream to "yook at duh ducks."

Without warning, he turned his attention to me.

"Do you think what you do makes any difference to those kids?" he said.

"Probably not to most of them. But I'm good at what I do, and I like it."

"What's there to like about it? You manipulate people instead of paper, or both. What do you make? Enough to mortgage your house where you'll stick 'til your kid has grown up and left you. At least we know what we don't want. You're a nine-to-fiver same as the grey suits on the buses. Take a look outside tomorrow morning when you wake up. Fog rolls in from the sea here. You can watch people scurry off to the salt mines and disappear like shadows until dark when they come back. Every day."

There's not a teacher worth his dedication, or his marking for that matter, who hasn't met and won't argue against the nine-to-five office worker characterization of his job. *Time to take inventory and fight back.*

The decade from the mid-sixties on brought heady challenges for a novice high school English teacher. Anti-establishment themes and alienated anti-heroes titillated young minds. Our students were well aware that south of the border cities burned and leaders were assassinated. Yesterday's wisdom was pulverized into tomorrow's conscience. Talk of psychedelic drugs was everywhere, a phantasmagoria of dare, double dare. Even the football team toked up before a game. No one survived unchanged.

"Listen. I'm doing what I like. I write my own courses, I teach the way I want to. I turned down a Headship and changed schools so I could be where the kind of education I wanted to be part of was happening. As for academics, sure, most of that is lost. But you don't teach subjects, you teach kids how to learn. And I like doing that."

Bev put down her book, Nigel Nicolson's *Portrait of a Marriage.* This was getting interesting.

"OK, so you like it," Hank condescended. "I liked wandering the back streets of Marrakesh. You like teaching in St. Catharines."

I almost said, "And when was the last time you were in Marrakesh?" Bev would have approved. But he had given up Marrakesh for Mirdza. I remained quiet.

I wondered why he was being so aggressive. Was he testing my defense for my benefit, so I could see if it held up? Was he masking disappointment with the flatlining of his own ambition? He didn't seem a man to welcome compromise, even if it came with a new family.

Mirdza rewarded me by attacking from another quarter.

"Don't you ever feel it's all a game you're playing with them? What can you teach them that they're really going to need? You don't know what you need yourself. You get your history books and novels and cram a paper world into them. They'll never see the real one. You come to visit us and go home thinking you've seen Europe, you know what it is to live here."

"We have no illusions about that," I defended. "And we're not raising world travellers in our schools. Most of them won't get jobs outside Ontario; many will stay in St. Catharines. They want what their parents have got, only sooner."

Hank saw an opening. "That's the trouble with you Canadians. You think the rest of the world doesn't exist. You've got all the answers, you and your precious three hundred years of history. How many of your students ever read Goethe, eh?"

"None. We don't teach Shakespeare, either."

"How about Knut Hamsun or Henry Miller?"

"We can't put Miller on the course. Anyway, they wouldn't read it. The stuff is on for its content, whether the kids can relate to it. Some of Hesse is on, *Siddhartha*. They choose their own titles. We don't teach any title class-wide anymore."

"Well, you go right on doing your thing, man. You and the rest of your smug little country. Keep thinking you know where it's at, what's happening. Hey, your little billy goats would like that, eh?" Hank raised his glass in salute.

"Why don't you think about teaching over here for a couple of years?" asked Mirdza. "You'd be getting out of St. Catharines at least. There's international schools that hire English teachers."

"I did look into CUSO. A friend of mine went to French Cameroon and lived on a mountaintop there. He taught math to black kids who wanted a European university education. It was a British course, set and marked by London, had nothing to do with those kids at all. They wanted an office job like a white man, and they'd do anything to get it ahead of their buddies."

"Of course. But at least he was living there. C. P. Snow's first rule of politics: Be there."

"Leave him alone," Hank cut in. "He wants to teach bourgeois kids how to be bourgeois parents. He can do that in St. Catharines as well as anywhere."

I'd met men like Hank before, chauvinistic by their own admission, egotistical, holding court as though they have God-given authority. I can get past the bluster if the spiel is worth hearing.

Hank, however, had run out of things to say. He relit a half-smoked cigarette from the ashtray, a sign that there was at least something he couldn't control.

"There's an international school at Neuchatel," Mirdza continued. "They pay your travel, and you get a good salary. You could work an exchange, perhaps. They speak French there. You could manage that."

I wondered what Bev was thinking. Another red flag, no doubt. In my mind, I had already rented out our house back home. That was significant. I had not sold it. What an experience for our son, Paul; four years old and a citizen of the world already. And the Matterhorn was in Switzerland, that aquiline peak in the Alpo commercials ...

The record had finished. Hank got up and switched on the TV. The station was broadcasting news in German. Although he hated the Germans, he valued their journalism over the Dutch and English-language stations. On the ottoman lay a few copies of *Der Spiegel*. Nowhere, I thought, would a German feel more alien than in Amsterdam.

Suddenly, Hank was at the TV turning up the sound. The news clip showed a crowd of angry youths massed in a square. A wave of soldiers in riot gear advanced on them. Cut to a police van, people being pushed, dragged, carried in. Blood trickled through fingers pressed against a face. The picture bounced, dived and cut back to the announcer.

"Damn fascists!" Hank got up, went to the bedroom and shut the door, leaving the set blaring its nonsense at us.

"Why don't you heat up some coffee?" Mirdza said to me.

She turned the sound down and went off to the bedroom. When I brought the cups out, she was waiting.

"It was a student protest at the Polytechnion in Athens." This was the time of the Cyprus trouble and the transitional coalition government. "Hank knows the girl who was loaded into the police van. She had a part-time job across from his office. You never hear what happens to people like that. Nobody is notified, nobody has any rights. They'll probably let her out in the morning. Depends how full the cells are. Some people disappear for years, or forever."

"Did he know her very well?" Bev asked.

"I don't know. He saw her a few times. I think I'll go to bed, too. Can you look after the animals?"

On the inside of the WC door, taped at eye level, an absurd caricature of Einstein stuck out his long tongue at me. I could hear voices from their bedroom. Hers was sometimes distinct, his low and muffled.

"What's the matter with you?"

A loud slap answered her question. She gasped and dissolved into restrained sobbing. In the WC, I pulled the overhead flush chain and beat it to our room. In the dark, as we lay on the two ticks brought from Athens, Mirdza's sobbing peaked and died, again and again. Then, the unmistakable sounds of bouncing bedsprings excited the sobs to hysterics. *My God, he's raping her!* I stopped breathing to listen. I was locked out, impotent, forced to acquiesce to this brutality. I was trapped on the train to Vienna again.

Finally, Hank opened the door and shuffled down the hall to the kitchen. I waited for her weeping to exhaust itself. I didn't hear him return.

Next morning, I busied myself washing up the previous evening's mess. I heard her behind me.

"Are you OK?"

She murmured something. I turned and looked into her face. Huge red circles crowded her tired eyes. The rest of her face was bone-white. In the light, in the time since Athens, she'd grown old.

"Can I do anything?"

She paced back and forth distractedly from the table to the fridge, opening and closing the door for each item she carried. I watched her when I could. She wore a frumpy knee-length robe that made her body shapeless. Her hair was greasy and tangled at the back, her shoulders heavy, bent over, and her calves looked rough and cracked.

Hank arrived late for breakfast. He complained once about his egg. The rest of the meal we consumed in silence, like characters in an Andy Warhol movie.

After breakfast, Bev convinced Mirdza they should take Melissa to the sea for the day. Bev was hoping she would get the full story, and Mirdza needed something to do elsewhere. Hank objected, and then gave up and spread out yesterday's *Washington Post*. I headed for the balcony with one of Hank's African collection, Chinua Achebe's *Things Fall Apart*. When the sun moved around to blaze the pages white, I moved inside. Hank was listening to a record through headphones. He closed his eyes and drifted back to 1953 on the Yonge Street strip, playing a muted trumpet behind Miles Davis on the Telefunken sound system. When the record ended, he got up to flip it, noticed me, and switched on the room speakers.

"He's a genius with a horn," he said. "I named my son after him."

I knew his ten-year-old son's name was Miles but hadn't made the connection. What ate at Hank was that he had no access to Miles. The boy's mind had been poisoned against him by his socialite pretender of a wife back in Germany. She had drained off his money and left him emasculated and embittered.

"Do you ever see him?"

"No. Terri and her bastard lawyer friend have seen to that. I've filed for divorce. She won't give it."

I recalled what Mirdza had written about Terri in one of her letters:

"She's welcome to try to get him back, but because she thinks they could have a good life together, not because she thinks she's *entitled* to it. No one is entitled to anyone else's life. I guess that's my beef against marriage, that it's just too easy to treat your partner like your dog, servant or prize stamp collection."

"All the time she's sleeping with the son of a bitch," Hank resumed. "You know what she told Miles? She said I'd shacked up with a black whore. Who else has he got to believe? She won't let him see my letters, she reads his before they go out. I don't know why he keeps writing."

"Can't you do anything to get custody?"

"I have. Every penny goes to lawyers. But you can't fight it from outside the country. You can't get a lawyer to care enough. I'm an ex-pat. I can't go back. Even if I did, it's the bum, belly and tits they listen to. Not a damn thing I can do. These women have it all their own way. You know what we need is fucking male liberation."

He slipped back into the jazz again, as though he didn't want to lose Miles in a stupid conversation on men's lib. I picked up Dag Hammerskjold's *Markings* from the lamp table and browsed Auden's introduction. Auden claimed Hammerskjold, Secretary of the UN, was just another martyr. The book's fly-leaf was inscribed "To Mirdza, from Margo."

"I guess we were pretty hard on you last night, eh?" Hank interrupted. "But you took it all. You're as straight with us as you can be. Tell me what you think of us, then."

I couldn't read him.

"I don't understand why you hurt someone you love," I said deliberately.

"Do I? You think so? Yes, I suppose I do. At least I get it out. She goes whimpering about like a little girl, and you admirers fall for it. Or didn't you know you weren't her only admirer?"

His redirection caught me off guard.

"There's a professor in Montreal," he went on. "He's a … what do you English call it … a fop. His wife's nuts, chronic depression all the time. He should commit her, but they won't take her. So he writes Mirdza these incredible letters, like you."

Hank had read my letters!

Then, with the bitterness of a man asking to be cuckolded, he continued, "You qualify if you glitter. Glitter is be successful, be interesting, be strong. Go ahead. Stand in line, and good luck!"

There was a knock at the door.

"You both have her up on a pedestal, and she loves every minute of it. You think she's some kind of intellectual, a free woman. 'Wilful' I think you said. Well I live with her. I see a little girl who hasn't cut herself loose from her mother yet. You think she wants to change the world. You don't know what she wants. She wants kids! A momma's tit, that's what she wants to be. If I didn't keep pushing her …"

A second, more insistent knock broke his rant.

"Ha! See, she's locked herself out."

Pleased to prove himself right, he opened the door. In the hallway stood a middle-aged man with a grocery box in his hands.

"Hello, Hank. I found her in the grass. Like this. There wasn't any sound. I felt her bones all over, they seem alright. She's held her head up all along, too."

Hank took the box and turned to me.

"What did you do with the cat last night?" he accused.

"Put it out on the balcony with the food. Why?"

Hank reached in and picked up the cat. Felix folded limply into his hands, his mouth open in a silent cry.

"There's no blood," he said, looking it over. "Bones seem OK." He pressed the belly and got no reaction. "It's not possible. Seven floors down. That's a fifty-foot drop."

Felix's miraculous recovery took several weeks. They measured his progress by his attempts to climb up the red batik. He never again reached the top.

❧

Shortly after we returned to Canada, they were wed. Mirdza wore an African-print dress Hank had brought back from one of his trips. Hank stuck to his blue denim suit. The witnesses were an old acquaintance from Elsevier and Schulamitt, an Israeli girl trying her luck in Europe. It was a church wedding. Mirdza carried Melissa down the aisle. Afterwards, they all went home and discussed who should control Palestine. Hank favoured the Arabs because of the two million who had fled, and because Schulamitt was in the room.

Through their letters, we began to realize the oppressive circumstances of their lives. Bijlmermeer did overcome them both. Hank tried everything to shake off the nursemaid mother-substitute role he felt forced into. Increasingly, he doubted that this waiting period would transition to a better life. Each day, the dark continent of Africa glowed brighter in his memory, and the perpetual grey winter of Amsterdam only deepened.

Mirdza turned more to her proofreading and editing, bringing the work home to her desk in the bedroom, so she could be with her family, she claimed.

Almost a year later came the suggestion of another move. Mirdza was again pregnant. The baby's name was to be Aviva or Marcel. She would have to quit work. Hank's work permit had expired and he would not be granted another on the strength of his visa. The letters hinted of mounting debts. "We're all trying to fetch water in a sieve," Hank wrote.

When the phone finally rang, I was unprepared. Her voice could have been from next door, so clear was the line. She was nervous and spoke quietly.

"We're coming to Montreal as soon as the baby's born. Do you think you could lend us some money? We've looked into every possible source, and there's no one. Could you manage, say, a thousand or fifteen hundred?"

"Yes, of course, if we can. How much, fifteen hundred or a thousand? When do you need it by?" The words came perfectly easily. At last she had asked me to do something.

The next day I borrowed $1500, $1625 with interest, and sent it through proper channels to a safe Amsterdam bank, one that was unaware of their debts. I convinced Bev that I would do this as a gift, that we would likely never see a penny of it again. The only other monies we gave out that year were two $5 donations to Cancer and Heart Fund canvassers, both of whom were neighbours.

It was almost a religious feeling for me. I was no longer confined on the train to Vienna, no longer listening helpless outside their bedroom in Amsterdam. I had been chosen, called to serve, given my part to play. They had already paid me back by asking for my help.

❧

In December 1974, they came to 1848 Rue Lalonde in Montreal's French-speaking east end with Melissa, now three, a four-weeks-old Aviva, Bismarck the dachshund and Felix the cat, who had become something of a living talisman to them. They reduced their belongings to a few boxes. The battered trumpet, the people tree, the carved masks, the jazz records, those will be with Hank until he dies. So will the photographs – the scene on the chesterfield in a Toronto apartment with Terri, some friends and an old black man from a blues band, the postcard of an elaborately decorated mosque, the snapshot of a nude Mirdza lying on her belly with the cat sitting on her back, its tail resting down the crack of her buttocks. His library was depleted to a few German editions, one or two Heinemann paperbacks of African authors in translation and a fold-out world map that looked as though it had fallen in with the laundry.

To me, it hardly seemed like emigrating. My own journey from England to Canada when I was a boy lasted ten days on a single-engine Cunard liner across an amorphous expanse of grey Atlantic, a severe traverse between two lives. Theirs seemed not so different from taking a bus to the next town over and finding a place to stay.

For Mirdza, returning to Montreal was coming home. Old and new, French and English, goys and yids, mountain and river – she knew them from her undergrad days at McGill. Her friend Howard found them an apartment, a windy top floor in an all but condemned tenement house for $60 a month. Each morning, Mirdza dropped off Melissa and Aviva at a *garderie* and bused to her downtown office. She could tour the whole city for thirty-five cents by riding the buses to the end of their lines.

Hank was afraid to choose a new career for fear it would reduce his options. He knew he would never have a second chance. He inquired about retraining as a cabinet maker. Once, he volunteered for an experiment at the university. They offered him $80 to pump some drugs into his blood, easy money until he asked what the chemicals would do to his brain cells. Then he refused, but was proud of his intention to sacrifice his body to provide for his family.

Mirdza landed a few freelance projects for *Southam News*, which bought her time to find a part-time job as editorial secretary to a Dr. Scott, a seventy-year-old psychiatrist who was committed to preparing a seven-volume opus of his life's practice, one volume a year. She found the work difficult at first, and he left her alone with it. Then she became intrigued by one case history in particular. A criminally minded patient had resisted all of Dr. Scott's attempts to regress him. Finally, the doctor started blathering to the man as a baby would, and a whole interchange of furious babble ensued. Child games followed, and then chess games, and the information slowly trickled out. The story fascinated Mirdza, and I think it led her to conjecture about her own childhood and what might be hidden there. Born stateless in a Latvian Displaced Persons camp in 1949, she did not know much about her early years.

The proximity of her mother and father also pulled at her. Melissa, she reasoned, needed grandparents like any normal child. And they had a right to see Aviva, too. Hank adamantly refused to allow them to go, but then relented when Melissa's pleading wore him down. We offered our house as a home base for them during their visit, and they made the trip to St. Catharines in the summer of 1975.

That trip home was a mistake for them.

The first evening, Mirdza's father, Willis, told Hank he couldn't understand how he could stay home and put his family through all this, and he should get off his ass and get a job. Hank shot back that Willis was an old-country bourgeois bastard who couldn't think past trimming the hedge. Mrs. Baltais pleaded with her daughter to bring the children and stay with them. Mirdza begged Hank to address Willis gently. Hank emptied his wineglass over Mirdza's head and telephoned me to drive him to the bus terminal. Waiting for the coach to Montreal, I asked him what he would do if she left him. He said, "Kill myself. I'd have to."

Next afternoon at our place, Mirdza told Bev, "I don't have to take this. No one gets treated like this."

A couple of twenty-minute phone calls and two days later, I drove Mirdza and the children back to Montreal. When evening came on, we stopped for coffee at a service centre and ate deep-dish apple pie with ice cream. Back on the road, Mirdza soothed Melissa to sleep, and talked about her sex life. About how she felt used, and how the romance had gone out of it. Sometimes she "wished there was more foreplay." Then she stopped talking about sex and started talking about schizophrenia.

When we reached Dorval around 9:30, we'd both been silent for a while. The road was lined with hotels and restaurants, some closed.

"We'll be there within the hour. Do you want to stop somewhere first?" I asked.

"Do you?" she replied, slowly.

"If you do."

We both knew it could have been anything – coffee, a last chat, anything – if wanting made it so.

"I think I'd better get the children home. They've got the garderie in the morning, and I'm pretty tired. It's been a good ride back, though, Dave ..."

The next day Mirdza's father called her. Mirdza found out that while we were driving, Hank was still raging. He telephoned Willis and told him that Mirdza had screwed some Greek friend while he was off on one of his African jaunts a few years ago, and hung up. Then he waited like a righteous father for the prodigal daughter to return, with their two sleeping children, their suitcases, his briefcase and me.

Things seemed to go along fairly peacefully after that purge. There must have been some sort of arrangement – a relegating of responsibilities and roles perhaps, agreed-upon safe topics for discussion. In her letters, Mirdza shared that she was being troubled by dreams. They had mothers and fathers and babies in them, and dead people talking back from holes in the street. Sometimes they spoke in English, sometimes in Latvian, sometimes in gibberish. She arranged through Dr. Scott to see a psychoanalyst, a neo-Freudian. Once a week she chatted on about her ideals, her abandoned career plans, the children, her nightly routine, and then came home and wrote down her analysis of the session. After three months of this, her shrink declared, "Your problem is that you're suffering from penis envy." That grabbed her for a few days. Then she wrote him a letter telling him that he was a latent homosexual and never saw him again.

৵৹

A year passed since that disastrous visit with Mirdza's parents. Bev and I fell into a cool avoidance regimen, fueled by guilt and blame. Daily acts of consideration mutated into heartless rituals. The few mutual friends we had, all heading into their thirties, seemed to be questioning the entanglements of their own relationships. The house became claustrophobic. To avoid confrontation, we sank deeper into our work. By November, we thought we needed a break from each other, maybe to force the issue. The day after Christmas, I stuffed my backpack and took the train up to Montreal alone.

In the winter of 1975, Montreal seemed an organized city. Everyone had a place and knew it. Rue Lalonde, for example, was the final stop for those whose only interest was the quiet despair of taping torn polyethylene storm windows and turning the chair from the window to the television and back again. Rusted car engines revved into late evening, though rarely did a vehicle move from its curbside home.

There is a photogenic charm about the slums. Washing lines, tiers of balconies with rotten boards and wrought iron rails winding down to the street, the view across to a neighbour's kitchen through a broken blind and everywhere, cats. But it's damn difficult, as Mirdza said, to feel romantic when you're wearing long underwear and wool socks to bed. And when the Sally Ann has no more donated snow suits, you keep your little girl inside and stay home to look after her. You can wait forever for the summer.

Once a month, the landlady stood at the bottom of the staircase and called out the tenants by apartment number to collect rents, her white '73 Mercury purring in the middle of the street for the getaway. But now it's midnight. Doors shut the blank eyes away and the city sleeps off another day's guilt.

Despite the heavy backpack, I was smiling as I climbed three flights of icy steps to their apartment, like coming home to loved ones after years of quarrelling. The door was unlocked but jammed with paint. Inside, the kitchen light, left on for my arrival, faintly uncovered the corners of the room: the wall of bulky coats and boots; the rough-sawn shelves loaded with grains, cultures and sprouts; Bismarck's wicker basket; the photos taken in the white Mediterranean sun, pinned above the passageway to their bedroom; the bedroom door left slightly ajar.

In the silence of midnight, I stood only yards away from her, like a father watching over his precious one.

I have never known a more pleasurable sleep than I spent that night on their chesterfield. She lay sleeping in the next room. I was where I wanted to be. How different from the night three years ago, on that agonizing train from Athens to Vienna, when I watched the hillsides flooding into the spreading space between us. Hating myself for not stepping off the train as it raced past the shepherd fires that dotted the hills like fallen stars. Hating myself for not holding her in my arms even once before the taxi pulled away from her door. Hating myself for the tears drying on my face, for the pain in my throat that almost made me vomit in that stinking compartment, and for the spectacle I presented to my wife, the stoic and helpless witness to this outrage.

☙

By now, Hank was taking courses at McGill in philosophy, then in philosophy of religion, and then specifically in Judaism. He took Hebrew lessons and weekly lectures from a rabbi, paying his way by student loans and tutoring a few high school students in German.

He had, as he said, "a desire to investigate first-hand what I see more and more as a grandiose hoax: Christianity." He had never been a Christian anyway, never been able to get down on his knees and talk to Father. He seemed drawn to the Old Testament God, the one who nearly murdered Moses and called for the sacrifice of Isaac by his own father. Here was a God of strength, jealousy and vindictiveness. As the lone wanderer, Hank had been an outsider in Black Africa, Greece, the Netherlands and now Montreal. He'd proved his expatriation from Germany long enough. He was practically a Jew already – all he had to do was learn the faith.

His dedication to learning was fanatical. For another $60 a month, he rented the empty apartment next door and set up a study there.

He worked through the night, catching an hour's sleep on the divan when he couldn't see the words anymore. He bought a two-volume condensed OED, the one with the magnifier in the spine. He kept his own dictionary of terminology unfamiliar to him. He asked Mirdza to read his papers and then tell him what he was trying to say, to see if it came through.

The routine demanded more of Mirdza, but the separation gave less opportunity for conflict. There was little humour but less tension. When they came together for meals, the table discussion was often excited, about whether Isaac was suicidal or Abraham was being punished for the guilt of those before him, but not about her failings and his expectations of her. Each found a life within the marriage that sustained them sufficiently.

Aware of this, they began to foster routine. They reasoned that if Hank was to understand Judaism, he ought to observe its ceremonies. She didn't keep a kosher kitchen, but for Sabbat, they baked bread, and before sundown they lit two candles and read from appropriate passages. They gave presents at Hanukkah instead of Christmas and replaced bedtime fables with Old Testament stories.

There was a structure to their days, importance in their activities and a sunny goal in their future. Hank's newly found success at writing university essays – straight A's in all but two papers – gave him the idea. He could teach at a university in the sun. The University of Kuwait was hiring English teachers. But for all his self-taught fluency in English, he still lacked the conviction that he could be a linguistics scholar. His Judaism studies, however, could lead to a post in any of several universities, or even in a Hebrew school. And he could work out one year of his studies in the sun-bleached city of Jerusalem.

❧

I awoke to hear Mirdza preparing breakfast meats and cheeses. She had not yet brushed out her hair, but she looked young again, a fresh twenty-nine.

"Hungry?" she said with a smile.

"Sure."

Melissa and Aviva were already into their food, but the end chair was empty.

"Hank's still asleep. He's finishing a paper supposed to be in before Christmas. I think there's only a bit of typing left to do on it, and then he'll be free. You came at a good time."

She took off her apron and sat down.

"You're well established here," I said. "Plenty of room, daycare for the kids, you're on your feet. It's been a long time coming. I'm happy for you both."

"Thanks. Actually, we're thinking of moving. We've got our name in for an apartment downtown. It's really not much more expensive than this one, and we could save on the buses. It's on Stanley Street, right between the campus and Dr. Scott's office. We could walk to work. That saves $2 a day, $60 a month."

"You must have thought it over. It can't give you as much room as you have here, with the two places."

"No, it's a two bedroom. Hank can use one bedroom for his study, and we'll sleep on the floor in the living room. We brought over those big feather ticks you used in Athens, remember? They'll do for now. There's other considerations, too. I used to think there was something special about living out here, in the French quarter, something real, close to the roots. There's not. We don't talk to people. Look at their faces, they all look like they've got some disease. I think it's time we cultivated friends."

"You've got friends. Howard, and Nikki and John, Margo, us."

"Of course. I mean people we can see whenever we want to. Not a few intellectual transients. That's what it seems to us, anyway. People we can do ordinary things with, not feel like we have to be profound. You know, I doubt Hank would ever tell you this, but he's never in his life had a male friend that he could keep. Maybe that's something to do with him, I don't know. I want people to come into my home and be normal. I think we've all been alone too long. There's something incestuous about it after awhile."

She gulped down the last of her coffee and prepared for the cold.

"Would you mind staying with the children until Hank wakes up? School's out, the garderie won't take Aviva in the holidays, so we try to take turns with them. I have to go into the office for the morning, but Hank should be up in an hour. While I'm gone, you can have a look at this if you like." She handed me a notepad from on top of the washing machine. "It's a sample for a column I'm trying to get in *Chatelaine*."

"Still your teacher, eh?"

"No, Dave. I want an objective opinion. Hank says it's crap, so anything you say will be okay."

The piece was a pedantic harangue about how women's sexual behaviour has always been a conditioned response to the expectations of the male libido. Women were incapable of thinking of their sexual activity as their own and saw themselves as receptacles for the male will. The final paragraph encouraged women to establish their own conditions of sexual behaviour. The prose wavered between scholarly restraint and a borrowed militancy, neither of which would endear her to the editors of *Chatelaine*.

"I hope you can talk some sense into her. She's a child when it comes to accepting criticism."

A frazzled Hank leaned against the door jamb.

"I don't bother anymore. I've spent half my life in publishing, and she won't believe me."

"Yeah, well, I know what it's like to get your writing ripped apart by your spouse. I don't trust Bev's judgment half the time, either."

"Look, when she gets back, I'll take you downtown to where the real stuff is. Classics have a remainder store there. Books are down to a tenth of what they cost retail."

The Classics shop was fourth on the tour of bookstores. At each one, Hank took me in to see the rare editions and chatted awhile with the proprietor, if he knew him, before he hustled me on out again.

"Hey, look at this," he said, grabbing my arm. He held up a massive tome called *The World's Religions*, produced on glossy paper with encyclopedic entries and luxurious colour prints. A $40 book, it sold for $8.95 on the remainder shelf.

"Fantastic, eh? Mirdza sent it to Willis for Christmas. Can you imagine what that ignoramus would do with this?"

He slammed the book shut and put it down heavily on the pile. On the street again, he pumped his short legs fast to get him through the cold. No matter what pace I struck, he'd walk a half-step ahead of me. Perhaps it was a habit left over from the days when it was his business to impress people. Almost home, he suddenly disappeared into a bar entrance, then emerged a minute later and took my arm.

"Let's have a drink in here. I hate these places, but there's something I want to talk to you about."

I wondered why he chose not to broach the subject at home. It was mid-afternoon and the place looked like closing time. Two girls moved in a lethargic angular dance to a French beat from the jukebox. Two men sitting apart at the bar watched them. The others were an old couple with nothing to say to each other, the barkeep and the waitress. We sat down at the farthest table from the dance floor.

"Yes?" In the semi-darkness, the waitress had still spotted us for *anglais*.

"Draft," said Hank. I nodded my order.

"Only bottle," she said.

"OK. Two Brador."

Beside our table, a large trap door flipped up against the wall. A fat man in shirt sleeves lumbered out of the black cellar below carrying a stack of beer cases. Over by the dance floor, the old man raised his draft to the two girls. There was no bottle on his table.

The woman returned, put down two bottles and glasses, made change for a bill and left.

"Bitch," Hank said under his breath. "No draft for the anglais. It's a wonder she even opened these."

"What did you want to say to me?" I poured my beer down the side of my glass and watched Hank pour his the European way, from a six-inch height.

"OK. I want to ask you something very important. I want you to make up your mind about it. Now, if you can. When you tell me, you must tell me the truth and never go back on your word. Do you understand? I'm too old to do this again."

He knew I'd be caught off guard. I nodded.

"You're intelligent. You can write. I want you to go on a trip with me. It'll cost each of us about $5,000. I want to go in two years, three at the most, to Africa. And I want you to come along. We'll see the real Africa, not the one laid out for tourists. I can take you places they don't even hear about. Back into the bushland. Up the Niger to Timbuktu – you didn't know there was one did you – then on to Ibadan, up to Kano and fly across to Addis Ababa, train alongside the Blue Nile and then by boat all the way to Cairo. If we have time, across to Athens, and from there back to Tel Aviv on a second passport. If the Israelis see the Egyptian customs stamp, they'd as soon shoot us."

He was deep into the weaving of his spell. I wanted to stop him, to get some breathing space. The names kept rolling off his tongue like an incantation.

"I can show you villages no white man has ever seen. An underground church with Greek, Moslem and Christian crosses chiselled into it. Cut right out of the rock. A university that's been there since the twelfth century, in the middle of the most savage land in the world. And the women in the cities. Did you ever wonder what it's like to screw a black woman?"

"Why me?" I interrupted at last.

"We have to pay for it somehow. Not while we're doing it, perhaps, but later, when we come back. We could write articles, features for newspapers, *National Geographic* and the like, with photographs. There's plenty of markets for it. It's the idea no one else has thought of, a journalist's dream. You could write a novel when you come back, an adolescent novel maybe. There's nothing for them, now. All it needs is a story line; the places will carry the rest. It's another world, and the experiences, God, you can't imagine it. Well?"

It was the fastest sales pitch I'd heard, and the only one that ever sold me. He knew the land and its peoples, and the ways to get what he wanted from them. He'd staked his life on this dream. I knew I could trust him with mine.

"I'll have to talk it over with Bev. It would mean a lot of changes. I'd have to quit my job, or get a leave of absence for a year. And she'd have to make do without me," I said, trying to gather reasons why I should turn him down.

"Damn it, man, it's not a life you're throwing away. It's three months at most, January to March to miss the rains. If you don't say yes now, you'll never get out from under, and you know it. What you've got isn't a house and security by the lake. What you've got is impotence by the lake. Get out. I'm giving you a way to try a whole new life, and I'm putting my head on the block to do it. You can always go back to St. Catharines afterward. If it doesn't work out for me, that's it. But it has to, Dave. We'll get a camera, maybe $500 for one, and not second-hand. One of us can take a course in photography, me probably. And when we come back, we'll lay out the articles – pictures, cutlines, heads and all – right across the editor's desk, ready to print, a package deal. What editor's going to turn that down?"

"When I get home, I'll talk to Bev. She knows how I feel about my job. I think I can persuade her. For myself, yes, I'll go. That's all I can say to you now."

He was not entirely pleased.

"You won't ever change your mind when you do get Bev to agree?"

"I've never gone back on my word yet. You of all people should know that."

"What can I say? I have to trust you." He stared at the foam in his beer.

"What about Jerusalem, and your studies?" I asked him.

"What about it? I'll go to Jerusalem next year, but then I have to come back to finish my degree. Trouble is going to be Mirdza and the children. The university can sponsor me, but they have no money for families. We were thinking of a kibbutz for them outside the city, but it'll be expensive whatever we do."

"Three years from now, you'll be teaching somewhere south of the Mediterranean. What of our trip then?"

"Maybe. I'm not a Jew. They merely have a more acceptable system of belief to me. I know I'm going to Africa. This seems the best way. I can't do it alone. Neither can you."

"We're in it together, then."

He returned my smile and drank his beer.

Later that evening, Mirdza brought out a Scrabble game. It seemed an easy way to fill time and didn't intrude on our conversation.

"What did you think of Hank's idea?" she asked when it was his turn to find a word.

"I think it's great. Took me by surprise, of course. I had no idea you'd talked about it together, either. Do you approve?"

"People do what they have to do," she said.

She spelled out TOTEM on the board and scored herself twenty-eight points. Hank fell behind and started chattering. He found the words easily enough but couldn't seem to get the knack of the scoring.

"You have the advantage over me," he said. "It's your native tongue. We should have Willis here, eh? He's an expert on four-letter words."

Mirdza looked away. I scored sixteen for my word and turned it back to Hank. He pondered over the letters, shifted them in the slot a few times and mumbled something about "Latvian consonants."

"I want this to stop. I'm getting very upset," Mirdza blurted out.

Hank pushed back his chair and went outside to go to his study. In the embarrassing silence, her eyes looked unfocused, like the eyes of a mime in a room of glass walls.

I saw the same tattered copy of *Markings* and picked it off the shelf. It fell open to a page about the middle of the book, where a thickly penned bracket marked off these words:

> Tomorrow you will have to play a much more difficult piece – tomorrow, when the audience is beginning to listen for wrong notes, and you no longer have me in the wings. Then we'll see what you can really do.

It seemed an invasion of privacy to read it. I put it back, and held up a large cartoon book entitled Kats.

"What's this?"

"A present from Margo. I have no idea why she sent it to me. It's quite stupid."

"Like giving your folks that book on religions. I shouldn't think they read much of that, either." It was one of those things you say because you've been thinking all evening that you mustn't mention anything about it, and it didn't last two seconds in the air.

Mirdza slammed down her hand on the Scrabble board.

"I wish you'd shut up about my folks, Dave. Just shut the fuck up!"

I could feel the blood race in my neck. My voice shook. "Look, I didn't mean anything by it. I don't talk about your folks. I don't even know them."

She damned me with her blank expression. Then, she moved slowly around the table towards the bedroom, turning in the doorway. She spoke, careful not to blink the tears from her eyelids.

"I'm sorry. It always gets back to my parents, and I've had enough of it. It's really got nothing to do with you."

I watched her close the bedroom door behind her. She would sleep alone tonight.

Sometime in the middle of the night, I heard her arguing fiercely next door. There was no audible counterattack, and soon she went back to bed.

Next day was Sunday. Hank had gone into seclusion. He had everything he needed, except food, which he was apparently willing to forego. Mirdza and I kept the children busy until mid-afternoon. Then, over coffee, she said, "He made a long-distance call last night." It wasn't an invitation for discussion. She was simply accepting the fact, and what it meant.

Soon afterward, the telephone rang. Willis's bi-weekly Sunday call. Mirdza spoke in Latvian, with the occasional English phrase, and then called Melissa to the phone.

"Hello, Grandpa," she said.

"Tell him you got the presents, and thank him for them," Mirdza coached.

"Fine. School's closed. It's holidays."

"Thank them for the presents."

"Mummy says thank you for the presents."

Melissa lowered the receiver to her waist, let it drop against the wall and ran to her room.

"Melissa!" Mirdza reached for the phone. She listened for a moment, saying nothing, and then quietly hung it up on the hook.

"Madness. I'm living with a madman," she said. I waited for an explanation. She sat down with that familiar stoic rigidity I'd seen her use when she needed time.

"He's on the extension, telling them their presents are going in the garbage. It's really not possible, is it? I think you're watching the breakup of a marriage. I hope he gets it over with soon. Two or three months, no more."

I reached my hand halfway across the table. "Maybe some people have to be married awhile before they can break up." It was a stupid thing to say, but it didn't matter.

I left for home that evening, two days earlier than the date on the train ticket. When I was ready at the door, she said, "I think it's best if we don't see each other again, don't you? It's too much for us to handle a long visit. We can manage an evening, but I guess we're not up to living with people for days at a time."

She frightened me. She was sure. I put my hands on her arms. "Will you be all right? What will you do?"

"I have choices."

"You're welcome to come and stay with us, for whatever reason. We've got room. You can live with us, get away for awhile, your parents wouldn't know. One phone call and I'll have you down the same day, you know that."

Her eyes gave a mercifully ambiguous response.

"Keep in touch. Let us know what happens. If there's anything...."

I held her close.

"Goodbye, then."

"Never say goodbye," she whispered into my coat.

I heard the door close behind me, so she would not watch me descend the stairs.

I wrote two letters after that: the first, a sort of query into what had happened during the visit; the second, a plea for some answer of any kind. The mails were silent. I never telephoned when cheap Sunday rates came around.

Holding On

Taking apart my MG bolt by bolt
is a winter preoccupation.
Ripping out carpet glued down since 1970,
the year I fell in love with Athens
and a girl who looked like Joan Baez,
and wept upon leaving them behind.

The carpet seems welded to the metal,
unwilling to break its 37-year bond
with the floor. It pulls up handfuls
of rust dust, and just by luck,
leaves no holes behind.

She e-mailed me today,
wants to get together soon,
before the car is fully restored.
They say when you fall so hard
you do not know the one you love.

She has denied all these years
any resemblance to Joan
until now, when a picture I sent her
reminds her of her youth
when she brushed her long hair back
and nursed her first born
in the Greek summer heat.
I put the picture in my album
after the MG insurance photos.

Canada is wrong for an MG:
no winding roads lined with hedgerows,
too few top-down days,
and then the killer winter salt.
I may not know where the bolts go
how to put Humpty back together
or what if anything the new interior
will change in the ride.

But when I'm alone and driving
along escarpment concessions,
careful not to lose the muffler
in the occasional potholes,
and my hair tangles and stings my eyes,
and the sun burns white-hot on the door rail,
sometimes, sitting beside me, there's Joan
singing *the green, green grass of home.*

Inches

The kid died on Christmas day. Lost his head. Decapitated. His van, cut off by someone turning in front of him – missed him by inches – wrapped around a hydro pole and put our power out for four hours. Families were gathered for dinner and presents, turkeys were half-cooked, driveways were packed with cars, and streets waited in the dark and cold. People would have cursed the kid and not the power company if they'd known.

It wasn't a kid. You'd normally think that, right? He was thirty-one, with family and a new address on Lakeshore. I read his name in the paper – Gary Carruthers. I taught a Gary Carruthers, I think, maybe fifteen years ago. A scrapper as I remember him, put upon by other toughs and willing to fight his way out of it at the risk of getting his head kicked in, or maybe it was only one punk and over a girl – it doesn't matter. He stood his ground and got beat. I liked him for that, not that we confided or anything. I heard about the beating from others in his class when he didn't show up. They said he was in hospital. I thought I should visit him, but I didn't. I had visited another kid in the Thorold Detention Centre, and I stopped by the hospital to see a girl with a brain tumour, but I never went to see Gary. Now he's dead.

One June day, after school, I was driving down Olive too fast, and I saw him on the sidewalk walking toward me. Like an idiot, I sped up to impress him, and he yelled at me, something like, "It's a school zone, don't you know there's kids here?" And I knew he had me. I'd fucked up.

Why do people do what they do? A girl I once loved used to say people do what they do because they do it. Cop out *cum laude*, I say. There's always a reason. Right now, I'm sitting here writing this after a beer and I'm on my second and I've been up all night and it's ten minutes to six a.m. and I'm looking at the Christmas cards strung out above the front window. I've even counted them before. Why do people send them? So they get them. Except Mr. Bean: he skips the middle man and sends them to himself. The Virgo in me used to keep records of who returned cards. Pathetic. Or maybe some people remember you fondly from some earlier life, work or high school or an affair, and they really want to make contact with you so as not to feel so alone or left or abandoned – like in kids' fairy tales, if you believe that psychobabble. And maybe a few of them would've sent you a card even if you hadn't sent them one first. But then the whole thing would simply be reversed and you'd wonder if they sent you one because they wanted one back. And then there's got to be a few who quit sending cards at all when the postage went up years ago, and why should you expect them to send you one when they don't send out any. But you do, right?

So I'm going to the funeral today. I don't know the family. I knew Gary a long time ago, like I said, one of a cast of characters in my grade ten General class. There was the all-night chicken catcher who slept on his desk; and the druggie whose hands shook all the time, the one I saw in the Thorold Detention Centre, in with the adult pervs because the juvie section was overcrowded; and the over-developed sex princess who wanted to become a porn star and wore a T-shirt declaring that, which I made her turn inside out or go to the office, over which she swore revenge until it dawned on her that her inside-out shirt attracted more looks than its message had; and the computer geek who couldn't write squat in an essay; and the poor sot who worked her tail off to get a fifty and carried books home and now checks out books in the town library; and the pimply faced straight-haired frump who taught Sunday School at the evangelical church as practice for Early Childhood Education. They wore their emotions on their sleeves, and I loved them all. OK, not like that. There's no *To Sir with Love* here.

I don't give a shit about being seen, though I'll probably look around to see who shows up. Who wouldn't? Talk of the town. I don't even have a morbid curiosity about how many in this small town suck on the teat of the *cause célèbre*. Hell of a fifteen minutes. No. Or, if all that is true, and who gives a shit if it is, it's not the thing. The thing is, he's dead for Christ's sake. His fucking head came off. My sister-in-law passed what was left of the van and all the flashing lights. She said nobody could have lived through that. No one did.

So there it is. Today I'm going to visit Gary. For a few months out of his life – life! – I knew him. I might cry some and try to make it so nobody sees. I don't plan to talk to anyone. I plan to come home and help with supper for my friends who are coming from Toronto to exchange presents. It is still Christmas. To Gary's daughters, next Christmas and all the ones after will be the day Daddy died.

What else? Well, there's that girl with the tumour in her head, she's of interest. She licked me. I'll get to that. When she was in school, down in the basement in Spec Ed, she kept going to Toronto for tests and operations, and every time she'd come back and tell me they had taken it all. She even had plans for her future, working with animals, I think, in the local pet hospital. She was a gutsy girl, and my grade nines put her picture front and centre on their Heroes bulletin board display, along with Martin Luther King, Jr., and Michael Jordan and Hilary Duff or whoever was hot back then. I asked her to come into my characterization class in Writer's Craft, to demonstrate how spirit and courage could be shown in actions, like a paraplegic measuring progress in inches (or like when Pacino yells in the locker room, "Football is a game of inches,"), and somebody said, "Yea, but isn't she in denial?" And I freaked on him, asking, "What right ...?" and so on, and yet it was an honest question. But denial can get you through, too. What good is acceptance to a fifteen-year-old if it means she's going to die?

Anyway, she did eventually get back home, after the hospital ran out of excuses to keep her. One day, about a year ago, she and her mother were walking past my house, and I was out on the front porch, and we had words, and she came up close to me and lifted up her hands, and I thought she wanted to hug me so I bent down, and she locked her hands round my neck and pulled me down farther, and then she licked my face, up the side of my cheek, again and again, wet and slobbery, while I was trying to break her grip to pull away from her, and her mother was saying, "Come away now, Bee, come away." And then we were a tangle of arms and hands, the three of us, trying to pry ourselves apart.

And later I kept wondering why the brain does what it does when it's corrupted, and was this her sign of affection or thanks, or her spit in the face, or did it make no difference to her anyway, only to me who didn't get that she was gone from herself long before her body caught up? She died a few months back. But it made me deal with her, the grip of her hands locked behind my neck, her tongue sliding up my face like a dog's. She got to me. She made contact, in front of her mother. Cut right through my panic. Hung on when I pulled away. And now, as I'm writing this after she's dead, I wonder about her mother, whether somewhere in her darkest moments she admits she is glad of her daughter's passing, relieved at being liberated. It doesn't make a difference to the love, anyway, glad or not. It doesn't alter the fact that her mother did not scold, but said in a gently insistent voice, "Come away, Bee, come away." Come away from human contact, you're embarrassing the gentleman. And maybe all the girl wanted was to hang on a little while longer, till she got tired of it. Then she could let go.

I went to Gary's funeral. The children cried, their mother cried. The minister said the "To everything, there is a season" bit, and when he got to the part about "a time to be born," a baby cried, right on cue, and his mother took him out. I didn't cry. Not that that's important. I had simply wondered if I would. I know what it's like to see the coffin pushed past you, inches away from your hand, down the aisle and out of the church. I guess I really didn't know Gary, not enough to cry over him, anyway. Still, it seems a shame, as my mother would say, all of it. A crying shame. Sometimes, life is a football, and the difference between whether it floats into your hands and lets you pull it in or slips off your fingertips is, well, you know. And whether you leave the field on somebody's shoulders or on a stretcher, the game goes on. It has to.

A Bitch of a Marriage

She's quiet now, this old bitch of a marriage,
the heart rapid in her soft hairs,
the leathered eyes fogged.
You can see she's starving
though there's food in her bowl.

Yet sometimes her ears perk
like the pup chasing its tail,
the sleek body darting and dropping
so fast you backtrack to catch her,
the paws spread to spring off again.

When you come in she no longer hears you.
Asleep, she warms the house from her rug,
her feet flick to runaway dreams.
These days you wave the door in her face
to tempt her to climb the treacherous steps.

She came with the house
before there were children
and hardly a bed.
You love the old bitch,
you rub your face
against her head.

One morning, you'll wake and see that she's died.
You hope to discover her body still warm.
To lift the stiff cold corpse would break you.

Movers

He, showing his strength, struggling on the end
of my filing cabinet, lead-heavy though empty, his
shoulders creased by the sharp edge

orders me to grasp the other end from underneath
and tilt it toward him – he knows how to lift
steel, he worked the summer in a fabricating plant,
night shift mostly, cycling home at 3:30 through
fog or rain or pitch of new moon, heedless at
fifteen and saving for a motorcycle, saving to
pay me back –

and as I heave the metal block to tolerable height,
he backs me up, across the lawn to the steps, and we
jerk the thing upright into this strange place
littered with debris from twenty years of husbanding.

A liquid bead falls from his chin,
pings the metal and courses
down the cabinet side toward me
shrinking and stuttering
until past halfway it stops
weak and staring
till it disappears the moment
we manhandle the brute into position.

Trying the drawer latch I say
In a couple of years I'll be helping you.
The drawer stays shut.
One of us has pressed in the lock
and I curse the stupid thing
that has connected us.

Getting Ready

"Getting Ready" developed from a dream and a poem. As a non-swimmer living atop a thirty-foot cliff on the shore of Lake Ontario, I sometimes dreamed of situations where I would pay for my fear of drowning. In one such dream, I stood naked in front of the living room window, watching the lake rise over the cliff and crash against the house. This experience expressed itself in a piece of "automatic writing," in which I described falling off the cliff at different ages. One evening at my workplace, when no one was around, I went into the main office to type a lesson plan on the electric typewriter and tapped out a nonsensical prose poem instead, as fast as I could type. The writing came without thought or conscious awareness. Later, under Joe Rosenblatt's tutelage, I used this writing to create a poem, "Reclamation," which became the title poem of my first book. In the subsequent story, "Getting Ready," only the setting of house, orchard and lake are accurately portrayed. The rest, as they say, is fiction. Sometimes memories, like dreams, can seem surreal.

❧

A boy once came to a cliff edge. Looking down, he felt a strange and urgent kinship with the swirling white waters below. He slightly raised his foot and leaned forward into free fall. He never hit the waters.

Margaret sat at the supper table, idly turning up the cards in threes. "The oil man came today," she said. "Ninety-five bucks for November. I don't know how they expect us to cope."

After five carded runs through the deck, the fourth column was hopelessly blocked. She had unknowingly caught the Jack of hearts in the sleeve of her fur coat. She only wore it to demonstrate her support for her husband's austerity program.

"Lil told me how Joe asked for nights for the whole winter so he can stay at the plant and they can keep their thermostat down to fifteen. Sometimes he phones her in the middle of his shift to check up on her. He asks her what the temperature is, and she puts down the phone and goes into the living room to see, and then comes back and tells him. I don't think they'll be together much longer anyway, not unless she gets a good lay more regular. You know what they need? A boy. That'd make him appreciate her. They're not like us, eh? Timothy?"

Her husband was stuck in the Naugahyde recliner, staring out the front window across the lake. Over his ears, the two cones of his headset bulged like black burls. Their pulsing had anaesthetized him into another of his after-dinner meditations.

"Goddammit. You've got the thing cranked up to nine again," Margaret said, jerking the jack out of the tuner. The record, *Also Sprach Zarathustra*, continued to rotate on the turntable though the tone arm had returned to its clip some time ago.

"Mmmm?" said Timothy.

"The oil man came today," she screamed.

"Oh. It must be the storms."

"What?"

"The night storms. Here, listen." He lifted off the headset and passed it up to her. "You can hear them building out there already."

A boy leaned forward in continuous free fall. The rushing air bruised his body and tumbled his mind. He never hit the waters.
Right before this happened, a fisherman, trembling and pale, approached the same spot. Looking down, he saw in the silver-sheen surface the expected image of a boy's face.

Timothy understood the power of the lake. For the past three years, he had been losing ground. Literally. His bungalow overlooked Lake Ontario from a half-acre treeless lot atop a thirty-foot cliff. Because of the earlier annual opening of the Welland Canal system, or excessive runoffs from heavier spring breakups due to global warming, or the increased precipitation resulting from undetermined atmospheric pollutants, the lake level had risen. When the winds cut across from Toronto every spring, the waves lashed against the clay base of the cliff and undercut the slope. The cycle of freezing and thawing further broke off the overhanging lawn edge, and a few more feet of land were gone.

Timothy never learned to swim.

He also never showered. He took long, hot baths. Margaret said the hot water would make him impotent. He said he did his best thinking in the tub. Really, he did it so he wouldn't get water up his nose. When he went under to scrub his hair, he squeezed his eyes tight, pinched his nostrils shut and locked the air in his lungs and cheeks. Sometimes he would play with the shampoo top, pouring water from a height and watching crowns of droplets form. Sometimes he would watch the light from the bathroom window glance off the water and dance like shards of the aurora borealis on the end wall of the tub. Sometimes he'd listen for the distant roar of building waves, and then he'd get out, lock the door and get back in to wait.

Looking down, he saw a boy's face.
"Many times have I held you in my heart," the man said fearfully.
"Many times have you slipped from me."
From the depths below swept a single silent whisper, "Wait!"

A point of scarlet beamed from the opposite shore.

"See that?" said Timothy.

"What?" said Margaret, stooping to pick up the Jack of hearts that had fallen out of her sleeve.

"The sun. They've trapped the sun inside the Toronto Dominion Bank. Do we have an account there?"

"No."

"I don't suppose they'll let us make withdrawals without an account."

"No. Maybe we could float a loan."

"Maybe we could float Toronto – over to this side. If not, would you stay here in this house with me?"

"Of course I would."

"Even if we couldn't borrow the sun?"

"Yes, dear."

"You could run home to your mother."

"That only happens in books."

"I read where it said that a man can own all the lands from sunrise to sunset, but he needs only a six-foot plot."

"I never thought about it, dear. Is that what you think?"

"I don't intend to die," said Timothy.

The fisherman, anchored on the shore, watched and dreamed of stepping off cliffs, falling into lakes, shattering the reflections of boyhood faces that waited so long to greet him.

Timothy awoke from a dream of three giant white birds with turkey heads, ostrich bodies, flamingo legs and eagle talons circling hungrily over his house. The noise of the waves roared in Timothy's ears like the constricted breathing of a dying man. He walked down the hall to the living room, nude.

Outside, the lake had risen. The lawn had become beach. The long, roiling waves that built from the lake's centre rolled across the surface in mounting swells and smashed in succession against the shore, the house's foundations and the plate-glass picture window.

Margaret, shaken awake by the house's tremors, snatched her fur coat about her and ran screaming into the living room.

"The storm's here," said Timothy. Draped about his neck were the headphones, which, along with several records and CDs, had fallen on him from the wall shelf.

"It's time to reorganize and move on," he said.

"Damn you!" cried Margaret. "Damn your fantasies, your delusions, your revelations!"

She pushed him aside and dashed through the kitchen and out the back door. Timothy watched her race down an aisle of skeletal peach trees in the orchard out back.

So did the three white birds. They dove straight for the muskrat coat. Halfway down, two of them smashed into each other and tumbled headlong to land in the trees like a tangled kite flapping in the wind. The other one fell on Margaret, drilling her to the ground with a *whomp!* Its talons ripped into her neck. When it rose up into the open sky, her fur coat slipped off and wafted down to earth.

"She said she would stay," he muttered.

He turned back to face the onslaught.

As the breakers spent their force against the foundations and receded, Timothy noticed three grey, chalky hills silting up where the edge of his lawn used to be. The house groaned under the pressure of each new wave, and the foundation blocks cracked and crumbled in sequence. Timothy saw between two of the hills, which were fast reaching mountainous proportions, a mile-long, fifty-foot-high tidal wave sweeping toward the barricade like the legions of God. It hit and levelled the two outside mountains, allowing the third to divide its waters. The bungalow felt the blow of a shattered sound barrier, snapped its one steel beam in three places and shifted itself free from its moorings as the water thundered over the roof.

Spread-eagled on the living room carpet, Timothy waited for the implosion of brick and glass. He looked up to see rock debris crash into his window and fly off through the black, watery space outside. He had the sensation of being in an elevator, moving up toward the mountaintop at great speed as the wave reversed its course. When the house broke the surface, the water fell away like a fountain. But the tip of the mountain on the edge of his lawn also broke the surface.

The house smashed against it, veering off again with the wave's current, leaving three of its basement joists on the mountain's peak for future aerial photographers.

In an instant, the waters swallowed the image.
The fisherman went away for many years, to prepare.

Reclamation

He was the first to build a picture window
shear off trees
leaving the tangling roots.
He trimmed the greening earth
and ferreted out weeds
with methodical madness.
The wireworms slipped deeper down their black holes.

Some white days, the lake became sky
and his world stopped at the cliff edge.
The water sucked sand
from under his feet
stole beneath the slope
cracked the surface
and a piece of his world was space.

On limpid winter nights
he slid down the ice banks
while swells slapped below
like a father admonishing an infant.
What stars,
silent eyes in a midnight forest,
plotted his possibilities?

He moved his chair to the centre of the room
when the wave gathered
like legions on the horizon line
rolling high over the water
a raw emerald curl
swallowing beach and cliff
crashed upon the window

and receded
dropping grey-white mountains on his lawn.
The second ice-blue force
smashed the glass
and spent its last upon his eyes.
Quiescent,
he waited for the ice to come.

Section Three

This House Is Condemned
for my mother and father, Valerie and Charles

Several key events during a lifetime can make you realize you are alone in this world. One is the day your child leaves the nest. Another, the day your parent dies. A third, though this does not happen to everyone, is the day they demolish your family home. Why these should matter isn't clear, especially when they happen in due course and not unexpectedly. Perhaps they mark the point at which experience becomes memory, or the point at which you have to cash in on your investment, take what life lessons you can and leave. Most days, these things don't seem that important anyway. Still, they are never far removed from us, for they have filled so much of our empty vessels and in large part made us who we are.

So, when I learned that the family home in Beamsville, which I had lived in for six years and my parents for forty, had been condemned, I began to sift through memories as though the place were as much a family member as any of us. I had gotten so used to driving past it when I went into town that I often didn't turn my head to look. Now, I expect I shall look at the empty lot and whatever development replaces it for a long time to come.

Our house was built 135 years ago from stones and trees, a clapboard-frame storey-and-a-half, white with shutter-green trim, supported by native fieldstone foundation walls. An oblong box, the house had Loyalist-style simplicity, the Georgian symmetry of a central door flanked by two bay windows and the Gothic Revival influence of a steep gable roof and modest brackets and cornices. Its beams were milled tree trunks, some with the bark still on, adze-hewn and notched to receive posts and joists in the manner of the stones at Stonehenge.

The front door opened onto a brief foyer just wide enough to accommodate doors to the long dining and living rooms on either side. A staircase rising between these two rooms led up to an odd panel on the rear wall of the house that looked as though it might have been a doorway to nowhere.

According to a tale our neighbour told us, the house once had another section of equal size extending at right angles from the rear. That would explain the phantom doorway. This half, he said, had been cut off and transported along the stone road, King's Highway Number 8, four miles to Vineland. I have yet to find any documented evidence of its move, but I did locate a photograph, dated 1938, of the congregation of Vineland Pentecostals at a tent meeting on the Beamsville Fairgrounds behind our house. The photo shows the extension. Another photograph of a champion Beamsville baseball team, dated 1958, shows the house as it was when we bought it, without the back part. Like the psychological wound left when twins are separated, the scars from this severance remained clearly visible for years on the gable roof and clapboard walls at the back of our house.

Time is a large part of what this is about. This typical southern Ontario house was my parents' first and only purchased home in Canada. When they bought it in 1961 for $8,200, mortgaged over ten years, it had already fallen into disrepair. Its two main rooms had been painted over in a garish deep turquoise. Their plaster ceilings were cracked and threatening to fall. My mother papered the walls, and a skilled plasterer shaped and swirled the ceilings. My father and I hauled Lockport Dolomite stone down from the Niagara escarpment to wall the driveway without mortar, like those English field walls he knew that have stood for hundreds of years. Then, we demolished the straight cement sidewalk to the road and set a gracefully curving stone pathway and front steps. On either side of the entrance, Dad planted giant yews, which in winter filled with bright red berries, and birds after them.

Our house was a work of our family's imagination. Any part could be altered to suit our interests. A potter's wheel stood in the kitchen, and a kiln was installed in the back mud room. As often as not, the kitchen table was covered with equipment for glazing pots or pressing flowers, the dining room disrupted by silk screening or wood burning or lino cutting or calligraphy, all hobbies my mother enjoyed. The television in the living room would run while my mother painted in oils. One day, I watched her as she sat in her armchair and painted the sky upside down because her arthritis was acting up and she couldn't reach across the canvas to paint it the right way up.

With us children gone, Dad transformed the dining room into my mother's House of Crafts. He made shelving from an old church pew he found in the basement of St. Alban's across the road, where he was lay reader. From this shop, Mum sold her little river-stone owls, her oil paintings of their pets and local scenes, her hand puppets, her silk-screened notes and the crafts she commissioned from several local artists. Town council took umbrage at the uppity notion of incorporating a business inside a house and tried to close down the inconsequential enterprise. They cited projected traffic congestion, lack of parking spaces and violation of zoning laws. The local press sniffed out the absurdity of snarled traffic trying to get to a senior's craft shop, and the council chamber gallery began to fill with curious spectators eager to watch the debate. The frustrated council sent a bylaw officer round to the house to insist that my mother trim her sign by one-half inch, which she generously agreed to do. In Leacockian fashion, the newspaper's follow-up stories made the council a laughingstock. The shop remained open as long as my mother wanted to operate it.

In those rooms, we listened to the sounds of *Don Messer's Jubilee* followed by the rapid-fire commentary of the *Friday Night Fights* on the TV after church choir practice. When she came home weekends from university, my sister and I washed dishes so we could spar with our inside humour and run through routines from Mike Nichols and Elaine May, or sing Tom Lehrer's Boy Scout song, "Don't solicit for your sister, that's not nice, / Unless you get a good percentage of the price. La la la …" My sister glued a poster of an Italian sea-cliff town over the ghostly doorway at the top of the stairs to commemorate her courtship by a British antiques dealer, whom she had met on a Mediterranean cruise – they exchanged love letters across the ocean for a year before he came to take her from us back to England. Sometimes, my girlfriend and I sneaked home from the high school down the street to neck during lunch hour. She became my first wife.

Customarily, my father would leave a book open in the house. It might be a coffee table book, such as the Book of Kells open at some illumination, or it might be his Bible with the black cord bookmark open on the TV table beside his recliner, as though he had fallen asleep contemplating its word. It might be a large-print mystery from the public library, past its due date, opened precisely before the revelation, its pages begging to be turned. It might be the black photograph album on the dining room table, opened to its tiny black-and-white prints of my parents' honeymoon at Torquay – my mother posed languidly against a boulder, the picture of youthful beauty in a floppy hat and long, flowered frock. Whatever the example, there was always another page to turn, another chapter to begin, another day to live, even when the reader had surrendered to rest – always more words waiting when the impulse to discover them returned. And if the reader in the house delayed, there were always others – visitors, neighbours, friends – to turn the pages if they chose.

It wasn't that he lacked enough suitable bookmarks or felt that dog-earing a book was unprincipled. I think it had to do with his knowing that for all he had lived already, there was something more waiting for him, some part of the journey to come that he had not expected, and he found comfort in this. I think he felt most alive when he was changing countries, changing his life, or watching the lives of those he loved change before him and knowing his hand was on them, the way a reader invests himself in a book and what is to come. A closed book is either finished or rejected; an open book invites promise.

As a hallmark of my upbringing, I was encouraged to carry out my own improvement projects. Sometimes, these adventures required the courage of youth, away from my mother's concerned watch. High ten-foot ceilings meant tall gables and a steeply pitched roof. Through gallon after gallon, my sister and I painted the wood siding and trim, me reaching too far for safety from the heavy ladder to avoid moving it so many times. To wire the TV antenna, I had to climb the precipitous roof on the rungs of an extension ladder hooked over the top, and then straddle the ridge as I clung tentatively to the rusted aerial pole. From that height, I surveyed the noise and lights of the midway rides at the Lincoln County Agricultural Fair in the Fairgrounds behind us.

One summer, to wind down after exams, I built a potting shed for my father. Later, he and I dismantled, transported and reassembled a greenhouse and fitted it with underground hydro and rain-barrel water. It ran all winter, a heating expense never deemed frivolous by my penny-pinching parents. To house the greenhouse seedlings, I made cold frames from pine-board boxes used to ship copper tubing at the factory that employed me one university summer. We never needed to buy anything new. If something stopped working, it was fixed or replaced with free-found materials or other people's castoffs. Parts of dead appliances piled up in the basement corners. Most problems could be solved by invention and time. A bolt could always be made from a rod and tap and die. We learned not to waste and not to want, to care for what we had and to use what was at hand.

My father's playground was his garden. Over time, with manure trundled from the Fairgrounds' livestock pens and horse stables, he worked the stubborn clay into a friable soil. Toward the back of the long yard, where the land sloped away and springtime water gathered in a shallow lake, he propagated rows of nursery stock and then gave the plants away for pennies at the roadside to make room for more. He experimented with standard forsythia, developed new hybrid roses and grafted an apple tree with a different cultivar on each branch. I learned how to prune trees here, to spur back growth to the first outward bud and shape the funnel of branches to let in the light.

The garden absorbed tragedy when it could not be avoided. On the Victoria Day weekend of 1994, my mother did not come home from the hospital. That summer, when others spread fireplace ashes on their gardens, my sister and my father spread my mother's ashes over her dedicated memorial flower bed so that the broom and heather that she loved would grow up through them.

After Mum died, my father soon lost his hearing and became blinded by glaucoma. Even before I sold the place to finance my father's care, the animals had begun to take over. During our time in the house, raccoons and skunks sheltered under the back porch; squirrels, bees and paper wasps nested in the attic; and birds, hornets and mud wasps lived in the eaves. In the fall, mice came in for warmth, and, while my father lived alone in the house, rats made their runways in the cellar. Thankfully, Dad's blindness and deafness prevented him from seeing or hearing the vermin.

Incidents began to happen that made it plain to me that the house was nearing the end of its useful days. The dining room, where as a young man I had argued existential philosophy against my father's Anglican beliefs and where, more recently, three generations of our family had met for Sunday dinners, now became a dangerous place in my father's wandering mind. Once, on arriving to check on him, I found him trembling in a corner of the dining room, convinced that he was standing on a narrow precipice high above a pit full of writhing snakes that kept him frozen in fear. On another occasion, his neighbour discovered him lying semi-conscious in the dining room doorway after having fallen down the stairs from the top to the bottom.

Bruised and disoriented, he may have lain there for hours. Even then, he steadfastly refused to abandon the home that had served us so well. When his blindness, deafness and terrifying delusions made living alone impossible, he was taken away in an ambulance. Leaving hospital months later, he took up residence in Albright Manor, a seniors' home near the escarpment, never to see our house again.

I emptied out the house, unceremoniously driving trailer load after trailer load to the town dump, and sold off the furnishings at a backyard auction I couldn't bring myself to attend. Everything we once valued, like the wooden skis stored since our childhood or the wooden ridgepole from our floorless army surplus tent, was disposed of. The empty shell was sold to a speculator for the land it stood on. Thanks to this neglectful landlord and his disinterested tenants, the house's decline accelerated. Shingles crumbled and blew off, the roof sprung holes, the windows were stove in. Horse chestnut roots backed up the sewage into the cellar, poisoning the house with noxious fumes. Time had run out.

The two principal threats to these century frame houses are fire and progress. Our house narrowly escaped fire when my blind father mistook the medium position for off on the kitchen stove knob. It did eventually succumb to progress. Smashed to rubble, it was cleared away in a day, its hole in the ground filled in and the land it once occupied, along with its neighbouring properties, now awaits the rise of some multi-million dollar development.

Many people could tell a similar story. This one is not extraordinary. Still, I don't know how to end this tale, because for me it has no end. The house is in my head. Perhaps when I die, the story will stop. And then where will my ashes be sprinkled?

Everything I Know about My Father

My father is a God-fearing man
During the war he came across a woman
squatting in a ditch
her body heaving
her face contorted
He stopped to help
but she spat and screamed curses
Later he passed her again
She was wiping blood from her baby's head
with the silk sash of her dress

He worked a morning in the greenhouse
preparing benches for propagating
and took the eleven o'clock train
up to London to fetch us home
When we returned not a pane
remained of the greenhouses
levelled where he had stood

The Jerries kissed the waves
of the Channel, swept
under the radar, over the cliffs
down on High Park
strafing the strollers
my mother among them
and circled back to bomb
in broad daylight
on Sunday afternoon

When I was four
I turned my tricycle
into the stagnant green slime
at the bottom of a bomb hole
and came up coated

I watched my dog
walk halfway across a road
turn to a double-decker bus
lie flat as it passed over top
then get up and go on his way
I shall tell my son of this
so he will know me also

End of a Garden Fork

The fork came with a guarantee, a lifetime guarantee. But whose lifetime? A Galapagos land turtle lives one hundred fifty years; a fruit fly, two days, maybe. My father, ninety years. Me, well, I'm still here.

Let me show you this garden fork. The handle and shaft are made of black space-age plastic glued around a steel core – no breakable wood here. The business end, the tines, was hand forged from a single piece of steel, stainless and gleaming as the chrome on a restored DeSoto bumper. The result: a heavy-duty digging fork like none other on this continent.

My father brought it back from his visit to the family nursery in England to give to me, a high school English teacher with no gardening skills or interest. I had spent my life listening to his encyclopedic knowledge on every aspect of identifying, growing and propagating any plant found in the UK and most of those in Canada, also. I had not processed a word.

True, when he drove to the Chelsea Flower Show to set up the nursery's annual display, his six-year-old son went along for the ride. And I had accompanied him to a Yardley's site in a bleak London industrial park (an oxymoron that delighted him) to cut a bed for annuals and set out a few foundation plantings that might give the place some semblance of a green, if pointless, oasis in a desert of grimy warehouses and factories. At age nine, in Canada, I had gone behind him and applied the elastics to secure the slip buds he had grafted onto rows of standard rose stock at Hamilton's Royal Botanical Gardens, but that was for money, an honest wage of 25¢ for a morning's work. But none of this education stuck. I learned more parts of plants cramming for a Grade 12 Botany test than in all my years of living with my father's expertise.

The day after he landed, he drove to my house ready to work in baggy brown trousers, a grey Harris tweed jacket prematurely consigned to garden duty – its sagging pockets bulging with pipe paraphernalia – and no hat, the hole in the ozone being a decade in the future. With a cat-that-caught-the-canary grin on his face, he presented me with the shiny new garden fork. It seemed more a trophy to be displayed than a tool to be sullied by dirt. He told me of its strength, its durability; that they didn't make forks like this in America or Canada; that if I took care of it, it would last a lifetime, as the guarantee said. He told me its price: $100, a small fortune for him in those days.

I wanted him to keep it. He would appreciate its beauty, its perfect design, its uncompromising strength. He would use it always. Besides, I had a fork, a True Temper® special picked up second-hand for two bucks, fine for turning sandy loam but useless in our red clay.

"No, it's yours," was all he said. "Let it do the work."

What work, I thought. And I took the fork.

That was sometime in my twenties. I'm sixty-nine now. Dad died twelve years ago. The garden fork outlived him.

Over the years, I brutalized that fork. Each time I tested it, it came up shining bright and still looking new, and so I subjected it to more reckless challenges not suitable for any fork. Finally, one tine bent, but did not buckle, under the weight of a boulder I was prying out of a hole dug for a small tree. The tines were no longer aligned. I clamped them together in a vise, but the steel resisted. I had to accept that I now owned a different fork, one whose left digit stubbornly jutted away from the others like an opposing thumb, but one no less capable of continuing to be my reliable helper in all things gardening.

An odd thing happened when I went to pick out the fork off the tool rack in the garage. It happened during a week that was unremarkable but for it being the ninth anniversary of my dad's death. The bottom of the fork fell to the concrete floor, barely missing my feet and leaving me holding the shaft in my hand. *That's that then*, I thought, *I'll have to get a new handle. Not likely to find a supplier in England after all these years. No paperwork on the original purchase, anyway. Well, it doesn't owe me anything.*

But when I looked down at the broken piece, I saw that the tines had not worked loose from the handle at all. The stainless steel hilt had snapped in two, leaving the top half of it firmly joined onto the plastic shaft. The forged alloy had given way of its own accord. Perhaps it was yielding to a history of unnatural stress; perhaps it finally succumbed to fatigue. It doesn't matter how I spin it. It's finished. And it went the same way my dad died: quietly, at rest – without me straining my weight on the end of it, flexing it like a yew bow, trusting it to hold steady and not send me crashing to the ground.

Last year, I took down a tall spruce and wrenched its roots out with that fork. You see, I have finally become something of a gardener myself. Now that my dad is gone, I want him to see my garden. I want to ask him questions: What will grow in this shady spot? How can I keep the hydrangea blooming blue and not pink? What will work on the mildew now that everything effective has been banned? I want him to walk behind me, point things out, show me how to plan. I want him to do all the things he did my whole life, things I had turned away from. I want him to talk to me.

As for the fork, the lifetime guarantee has been fulfilled.

The War Effort

My friend of forty years has a new job. It pays little: $12 an hour, down from $23 at her former workplace in St. Catharines. Niagara Machines used to make transmission parts for GM cars. Her output was fifty thousand parts a week. No one in 2009 sells fifty thousand cars a week worldwide. The plant closed in April, putting everyone out of work.

She survived on EI for a few months. Her divorce still isn't finalized. Her husband's name is on the mortgage, but he can't, or doesn't, pay. She has taken in a roomer who lives in his own mess and shares the house's facilities with her. She might have to take in another.

Some days, she picks up her granddaughter at daycare. The young girl is in Junior Kindergarten in the morning and daycare in the afternoon. It's a long day for her, but she loves the other children's company and often doesn't want to leave.

A few months after the layoff, word came down to the ex-employees with distinct skill sets that a shop in Belleville was hiring. She went on spec, signed on for part-time, found a room where she could stay three nights a week and began the weekly commute three hundred kilometres by bus to work. She says now that she is employed by contract, or self-employed, she has to keep working at this job. EI has stopped her claim because they consider this back-and-forth to be full-time employment.

One night close to Christmas, a young man in the bus terminal stood up and called out to everyone there that he needed $18 to pay his ticket home. He wasn't shaking and showed no signs of drink. My friend says she doesn't usually give to beggars, but on this occasion, she gave her last $15 to the man. She never knew whether he found his way home.

Her old dog and best companion has developed an eye infection. The eye shows blood and swells to a bubble. Vet care is out of the question. Each night, my friend holds the dog's head in her lap and washes the eye with a saline solution she has made. She says this helps, but her weekend work away from home causes the infection to grow again.

Did I mention that she makes bullets now? The .50-calibre ammo, each round as long as a pop can, is sold to the British forces on contract for sniper rifles and for "the workhorse of the British army," the "50 Cal" Browning machine gun, which fires six hundred rounds a minute. A single bullet can pierce twelve inches of steel plate used on armoured personnel carriers or punch a hole through a two-foot concrete wall. On a plain in Afghanistan, from two kilometres away, one bullet can cut a man in half at the waist. Since the bullet travels at three times the speed of sound, the man would not hear the shot that killed him. I imagine him dropping in silence, a pink spray raining up.

Forgiven

The day I heard my sister died, a butterfly leaped and hovered,
climbed the glass, landed on my jean jacket shoulder
(the butterfly, the first of the year; my sister, the last of my family).
I walked my visitor to the car and stopped, and waited.
Sheltered from the huzzah of wind, it opened its wings, breathing light,
flared its red ribbon against my denim. I sensed its raspy feet
as though, reluctant to leave, it wanted to carry me too,
as she did when we were children in the same morning bed
and our dog had been killed on the highway and gone to heaven
and was watching us make up stories and cry in each other's arms.
I didn't notice the moment it let go, bobbing and weaving up over the roof
as though it had never touched me, once a boy chasing butterflies
through weed fields to pin and set in their chloroformed death mask.
Back then I learned you must kill beauty to keep it. This day we parted ways.

April 18, 2012

For My Friend Who Grows Peaches

I stopped by to trade
a poem for a peach
knowing these hurried words
are culls
useless as the shock of waste
to you, riding
down aisles of old earth
your wrinkled fingers wrapped
round the wheel of the world
understanding the demands
of soil, limb
sky, leaf
and seasonal relations
with living things

you with the feel of
a peach in your hand
full round, easily
bruised like marriage
whose bloom comes away
on your fingers
when you grasp too tight
a peach cradled
in your long hand
a planet in the air
it was born to

It's a matter of timing
of predictable surprises
winter kill, blossom set
parasitic infestation
drought and canker
pick and pack and
come inside
proud of your acquaintance
with the secret life of trees
suspicious of the return
of other verities

So I'll keep my poem
and eat the silent fruit
you hand me

George and Gracie

A difficult story to write, this one began when a dear friend of mine passed away. A brilliant autodidact, he seemed to live several lives – some real, some in his head. I wasn't sure how to honour him, so I wrote this story. I think he would enjoy it.

ες

George sprawled uncomfortably across the computer keyboard. He liked the way his fur crackled as it reached up toward the warm monitor. He was watching Gracie clench her claws into Terrence's hair – right foot, left foot, right foot, left foot – working her muscles from her shoulders down through her paws, spreading her pads with each pass. Off and on, she had kept this up for the past twenty minutes, without a stir from Terrence. Terrence was not waking up.

George sensed that today was going to be different. Maybe today, George would jump onto the balcony rail fifteen floors up and leap out into open sky after the seagulls of his dreams. George the daredevil, the high-flier, the hero.

Gracie was getting hungry and seriously worried. She had never before been faced with Terrence's complete disinterest. Already she had cried, then wailed, then reversed tactics and, purring loudly, brushed her cheek against his. Nothing irritated him. Desperation overcame her. Her claws tore at his scalp as though she were sharpening them on the carpet-covered scratching post. Her mad obsession brought George back from the brink of imagined flying.

Terrence lay prone on the floor near his unmade bed, his pupils grossly dilated, his chest still as stone. Only two hours before, he had fallen, a solid, heavy lump, though to George and Gracie, both startled awake from a nap, it now seemed much longer.

"Gracie the worrier. Like that's going to get her anywhere," George thought.

"Am I the only one doing anything about this?" Gracie countered.

Behind George, Terrence's monitor displayed recently declassified CIA documents, *The Family Jewels*. They described several clandestine attempts on Fidel Castro's life, orchestrated by Chicago mobster and former rum runner John Roselli. Among the names listed at the bottom of the page was *T. Esterbridge, Fixer*.

෨

When American draft dodgers drank at his favourite bar in the seventies, Terrence liked to say he had been in 'Nam, just to jack them up. Terrence had done his homework. He'd seen both *The Deer Hunter* and *Apocalypse Now* in the first week of their releases. He could inhale "the smell of napalm in the morning." He researched the working parts of an M-16. He picked up the *Life* photo spread of the My Lai massacre and imagined the sights and sounds after Lieutenant Calley's soldiers had emptied their twenty rounds indiscriminately into the women, children and old men huddled in the ditch. How when they stopped to reload their magazines and heard the screams their first volleys had caused, they silenced the terrible din by firing off the second clip. Terrence's mind worked like that. He could convince anyone that he had been there. Like Gong Show host Chuck Barris, claiming to be a spy for the CIA. And if regaling his squirming audience with falsehoods didn't work, at 6'6", Terrence could stare down most threats. If he had to clock someone, his fist, about the size of a third baseman's glove, would decide the matter.

His other passion besides US politics was pharmaceuticals. Not in high school, when hash and acid and shrooms and blow were plentiful. Later on, after the flower power drug scene had gotten old, and the powder and pot new again. He became the tenement's drugstore cowboy, singing the Oxycontin Blues. He seemed to enjoy inflicting cumulative damage upon his body. "Narcoleprosy" he called it.

Terrence's professional career, which he thought of as his cover, was in reconstruction and restoration – an adequate description for what usually occupied his personal life, as well. He supervised the removal of the old church steeple from St. Aidan's on James Street in the heart of the city and laid the decapitated spire on the grass beside the flying buttresses, where it stayed for months. People passing by guessed that the wind had toppled it. They praised God that it hadn't fallen on someone or smashed into a thousand pieces. One couple actually went back to church because of the miracle. Eventually, when a fortuitous bequest from one of the departed faithful reinstated funding, Terrence had the fractured stone stabilizers replaced, sub-contracting the job to The Steeple People, who specialized in such work, and hauled the spire back up. The congregation thanked him with a framed etching depicting the erection of the spire, which he proudly hung in his hallway, near George's and Gracie's litter boxes.

Terrence's business contacts put him in touch with the City of Hamilton's major building contractors, some of whom were connected through the Musitano outfit to the Rizzutos after John Papalia was whacked. Through them, he believed he could reach the New York families, then the Miami mob, and on from there to penetrate the Cuban casinos. As a Canadian, he considered himself a desirable acquisition for the CIA, a foreign operative offering perfect deniability.

❧

Assassination is thuggery. There's no blow dart with the sting of a mosquito bite that brings down the victim days later. There's no Mata Hari pouring powder into a martini. The Company learned that lesson in 1961 when the Bay of Pigs went south. Two attempts to kill Castro had to be abandoned the same year that Oswald visited the Cuban embassy in Mexico City before he shot Kennedy. Six poison pills were retrieved and returned to US soil. Terrence said, "Never send a pill to do a man's job."

Thuggery is Che's desecrated body riddled with bullets, Kennedy's head blown apart, Lord Mountbatten exploded into smithereens. It's James Earl Ray bragging about his kill shot in the Silver Dollar Tavern on Spadina Avenue. It's carried out by pathetic loners and lower echelon lackeys who know nothing of the context or consequence of their contract. To the CIA, it only made sense to recruit mob hit men to do the deed. And someone untraceable to hook them up.

For God and country, neither of them his own, Terrence offered his services as a fixer. He did this online. He had already bookmarked the URLs of the White House, the American military, the FBI, Jack Anderson's columns in the *Washington Post* and CIA documents declassified in 1977 and 2007. Messaging into the CIA void, he declared that one dead Castro was as good as another, Fidel or Raul, and laid out what he could do for them.

This message was minimized over the CIA *Family Jewels* document that George's belly had accidentally opened on the computer screen.

෴

At the end of the second day, Terrence's body was cold and stiff. The night before, George had climbed onto his chest, walked around in a circle twice as though softening a bed of pine branches, and curled himself up in a ball. He was comforted by the smell of Terrence's shirt, a distinct odour as familiar to him as his own litter box, though the latter's odour was not distinct to Terrence. Terrence had lost his olfactory sense as a side effect of his diabetes. He often asked visitors if they smelled anything unsavoury in his apartment that he should deal with, meaning, of course, the cats.

George had always believed that his box was unique to him, but as he aged, he conceded that it smelled no different than Gracie's. Still, each one kept strictly to their own, and neither ever trespassed on the other's private collection of treasures. Living together, they worked these things out. Routines formed and roles emerged, either by mutual agreement or by George's decree. That's what big brothers were for.

George drank from the toilet. Gracie, smaller and more timid, would stretch up to the porcelain rim and longingly observe the cool, clear, life-saving liquid below. Fearing the bowl to be a slippery slope to drowning, however, she couldn't bring herself to step down into it. George, his thirst quenched, seemed unconcerned. His hunger was making him angry at Terrence for refusing to fill his bowl. "It's been two days," George thought. "If you don't get off your ass and feed me by morning, I'm gonna turn you in. So help me, I will." It wasn't a practical ultimatum, but George felt in command again.

ↄ

Wednesday, Day Three. The bowls were empty, the sand clumped to the max. George considered charging Terrence with neglect. *Abuse, yes, always good.* And there was the CIA thing if necessary.

Gracie noted that Terrence hadn't moved for three days. He was changing, becoming less himself. She didn't want to go near him. She began to suspect that the fetid odour that permeated the apartment might not be emanating from the litter boxes. Her stomach had tightened into an aching ball. George was urinating where he should not. Things were unravelling like a patterned sweater being clawed apart.

ↄ

Halfway through the fourth day, people came. Gracie heard a key rattling the lock and scuttled under the bed, inches away from Terrence's foot. George hid by the refrigerator, processing the sounds and what they might mean.

The door opened. Gasps of revulsion came from the hallway. Someone called out, "Terry. Terr. You alright?" This person was followed by the building superintendent, whom George and Gracie had hidden from before. Pets were not allowed in the building.

"How did you know?" said the super, covering his mouth with his sleeve when they found the body.

"I didn't. I phoned him when he didn't show up for work three days ago. I left a message to call me back. I've been thinking about it ever since."

"Better call the cops," said the super. They locked the door behind them. The police arrived within the half-hour.

"No sign of trauma," said one of the suits. "Get someone here who can pronounce. Get the coroner. And seal the place."

That afternoon, neighbours gathered in the hall whenever the elevator pinged. Terrence's sister found the door strapped with yellow police tape. She begged to be let in.

"You can see him at the morgue," said an officer. "We need to keep the scene pristine until the coroner ascertains cause of death."

"When will that be?" she pleaded through her sobs. "He has cats, you know. They need food."

"Sorry, ma'am. You'll have to wait for the autopsy. For all we know right now, this may be a crime scene."

"But can't I slip a bowl of food around the door?"

"No ma'am. Like I said ..."

∽

That was Thursday. Early Friday morning, a man and a woman arrived with a gurney and a long, black body bag. Twenty minutes later, Terrence had left the building, and his two children, behind.

On Monday, the death certificate said "Natural causes." The doctor's report concluded that Mr. Terrence Esterbridge had died from a coma induced by brittle diabetes. In conference, he explained to Terrence's sister and mother that this was a rare and very unstable form that afflicts only one in a hundred diabetics.

"You can monitor your sugar, take all the meds and stay on diet, and still your sugar can spike for no reason. Given Terrence's earlier lifestyle, there's nothing more he could have done to help himself," the doctor told them.

❧

Terrence's mother, Shelagh, had two cats of her own at home. But she couldn't turn family away, and George and Gracie were Terrence's family. By evening, when she returned to the apartment with carriers for the cats, Gracie was badly dehydrated. Too weak to stand, she went limp in Shelagh's hands. Shelagh could feel her trying to purr, softly, intermittently, a remembered reflex to being touched.

George decided he wouldn't miss the TV. He preferred an aquarium anyway. Fish never swam off-screen. You could count on them being somewhere in there the next time you looked. Pretty little snacks. If only Terrence had kept his tank, Gracie might still be all right.

George looked over to the balcony rail and the open sky beyond. The gulls had gone. A single star broke through the deepening night. That and a full moon closer to the horizon, encircled by a faint halo, were an oasis of light in the fragile canopy spread out across the smoky bay.

He turned to Gracie in the next cage.

"Say goodnight, Gracie."

Section Four

A Lakefield Summer Day

Having left Grimsby for Lakefield at 9:30 a.m. to avoid the Friday cottage traffic, I arrive in this sleepy village of twenty-five hundred people in the heart of the Kawarthas at noon. I have six hours to kill before the blessed event that I have come so far to enjoy: readings by two East Coast novelists, Sheree Fitch and Donna Morrissey.

My first stop is the Chamber of Commerce info centre / cop shop. A short lady with horn-rimmed glasses peers out from behind the tall counter.

"Can I help you?"

"Well, yes. I've got six hours to kill and I'm looking for something to do."

"You're in luck. We have the Lakefield Literary Festival this weekend."

"I know. It doesn't start for six hours."

"We have a strong literary history here," she continues, undaunted. "Susanna Moodie and her sister, Catharine Parr Traill; Isabella Valancy Crawford; Margaret Laurence – they all lived and wrote here. You should explore the exhibits down the road at the Christ Church Museum. Miss Laurence's house is just across the street."

"Yes. I met her some thirty-odd years ago," I said. "She smoked all through her reading to my students ..."

"And then there's Fiesta Buckhorn if you like wine and beer. Take the booklet with you. It's very well done. Professional. Glossy paper. Very classy."

"Any hiking trails?"

"Oh yes, The Gut. Wonderful waterfall there. It's about three hours' drive round trip."

Farther afield than I wanted to travel.

"And the Petroglyph Park. No trails there though."

"How about a cheap fish dinner?" I capitulated.

"Cheap?" She obviously hadn't heard this word from a tourist to Lakefield.

"Inexpensive? Reasonable?" I corrected.

"Well, there's Debbie's Lakeland Diner, if you like that sort of thing."

I heard *Darlene's Diner* and mentally archived it with *The Gut.*

‽

The curator of the museum-in-a-church, a senior citizen in a red golf shirt volunteering as today's host to the weary visitor, was shorter, and jollier by far, than the Chamber of Commerce lady. He was, however, locked out.

"I'm supposed to show you around," he said from the park bench. "I'm just waiting for the key."

"Ah. I'll have a wander then, shall I?" I said, already heading for the graveyard.

Not all of the early settlers buried there went gently into that good night. The stone of Anne J. Reed, who died in 1877, bears the inscription:

In death's cold arms lies sleeping here
A tender parent a companion dear
In love she lived in peace she died
Her life was asked but was denied

As a child, I'd often asked God for more toys and been told by my parents, "God hears every prayer, dear. He just says no sometimes." Too bad for Mrs. Reed.

"Tom Hanks has a place up on Stony Lake," said my smiling, erubescent host an hour later. "He likes us Canadians. He says he can come into town to the IGA just like a normal person here. We don't make such a fuss over our celebrities as the Americans."

I wasn't sure when Tom Hanks became our celebrity.

"And Margaret Laurence? How was she accepted in the town?"

I was fishing for some juicy scuttlebutt about her drinking binges or her decision to take her own life to avoid the further indignities of her lung cancer when, as she wrote in her journal hours before her death in 1987, "My body has become a damn nuisance."

My gentleman standard-bearer was not so forthcoming.

"She fit right in. No one paid her much mind. They do now, of course. Oh, there was that fuss with the school board about her book, *The Diviners* I think, but we didn't get too involved. Budge Wilson is giving a talk about her after the service in the United Church on Sunday as part of the Festival, if you're still around. That was her church."

"Yes, I know what you mean about not paying attention to her work. I was in a pub in Laugharne once, talking to a fellow who had known Dylan Thomas – he could point out his bar stool – and he was quite surprised to hear that Thomas was a poet, let alone Wales' greatest poet. To the locals, he was just a bellicose drunk."

My guide's eyes glazed over in a *What are you talking about?* look. I stopped myself short before launching into my best tale that the Welsh gent had told me, about bringing Thomas' coffin back home from the docks and stopping at every pub along the way, showing the corpse in the back of the wagon to any patron willing to buy their drinks.

On the museum wall, I discovered a chart that traces the progeny of Thomas Traill and his two wives, the second being Catharine Parr Strickland, Susanna Moodie's sister and Colonel Thomas Strickland's daughter. One of Catharine's nine children married an Atwood. Another married a Purdy. Had the entire literary galaxy of this country paid their dues in Lakefield? The jolly warden knew of no such connection, though I'll bet Peggy and Al had checked it out.

❧

Darlene's Diner, a.k.a. Debbie's Family Restaurant and Ice Cream Parlour, is empty because it's now 2:30 and the all-you-can-eat fish and chips doesn't start until 3:00 p.m. No exceptions. The chef is on hourly wage. Darlene, or Debbie, is a big lass, tall and large in frame, a force to be reckoned with. She asks me if I want to sit and wait the twenty-five minutes to chow time, and I thankfully accept. Two ladies come in, see me at what turns out to be their favourite window table and leave, promising to return later, presumably after I've gone. Since we are all on the clock here, that isn't going to happen. Not wishing to offend the locals, I move to another table.

The ladies return, accepting my selfless gesture with embarrassed smiles, and order the fish. Alaskan pollock isn't high on my list of edible fish, slipping in somewhere between carp and catfish, but Debbie swears by the cook, and anyway, she says, "It's what we serve."

Debbie asks the ladies where they're from, my first indication that the local regulars are neither local nor regular. But then, neither is Debbie as it turns out.

"I lived in Hollywood for years, the bottom of the pot," she offers. "Then Miami, and when I couldn't take that anymore, I moved down to the Keys."

"So, are you American or Canadian?"

"Oh, Canadian," she replies assertively. "My son was born in South Carolina." And the ladies, who are not from here either, accept her point. I'm reminded of the Irish line, "Everybody over there's over 'ere."

I've been browsing place names on the map in the classy glossy Buckhorn booklet. Several attach a natural formation to a family name, as though implied ownership rewarded one with settler status. Nogies Creek, Flynn's Turn, Crowe's Landing, McCracken's Landing, Young's Point, Hall's Glen, Burleigh Falls. I couldn't decipher the pecking order of bragging rights for a turn, a point, a glen and so on, though some lakes were dead giveaways: Upper and Lower Buckhorn and Chemong Lakes, Big and Little Bald Lakes. A blatant attempt to jazz up a most unfortunate family name, I assume, is Centre Dummer. Who lives there?

Then there are the animal lakes: Loon, Gull, Wolf, Pigeon, Beaver, Turtle, Sucker, Salmon, Sturgeon, Serpentine. And the lakes that describe themselves: Bottle, Clear, Cloudy, Stony, Sandy, Gold. And the aboriginal names, much more fun to say out loud, like a Dennis Lee poem: Catchacoma, Katchewanooka. Finally, the odd names that defy categorizing: Bobcaygeon, whose dark skies sealed Gord Downie's reputation as a songwriter; and Lovesick Lake, on which, as in Centre Dummer, I couldn't imagine anyone wanting to own a cottage.

The fish is edible after all, though with all these lakes and rivers around, I wonder why they had to go to Alaska for it.

As I return to my journal jottings, I am quickly spied by the culinary dominatrix who is my server.

"Doing your homework?" Debbie asks.

"Something like that," I grumble.

"Oh," she says in a *You're one of those!* sort of way. How many other uninspired writers have foisted themselves upon the literary ambiance of Lakefield?

"I always wanted to write a book," she continues. "I'd need a computer I can talk into. I'm much too lazy to type it all out myself. Wanna hear the first line? It's 'So you asked me to write a book, didya?'"

"Catchy," I say, and fold my tent.

෨

Both the Traill and Laurence houses are well kept by their present owners, though perhaps somewhat grudgingly. Lakefield prides itself on its literary treasures, though neither home is the kind of shrine to great writers that one finds throughout the UK. The Traill house, in particular, commands a view of the Otonabee River from its perch on higher ground that would have given its modest size a preferential aspect, were it not for the Trent Waterway System's derelict shed and stockyard at the water's edge. The judge who now owns Westove, the house where Catharine Parr Traill spent the last half of her life, fought against restrictions on changing his property beyond the spirit of the original structure. The judge will live out his days a victim of that Canadian habit of transferring ownership to those who came before: "Oh, you live in the Traill house." He can't renovate the house that will never be known as his anyway.

Farther down the road from Westove is a ball diamond and a large marsh with paths and boardwalk decks and raised viewing platforms for observing wildlife. A family of ducks owns the boardwalk, and a heron at the edge of the rushes took flight before I could lift my camera. The wetlands extend for miles, and kingfishers, buffleheads, mergansers, redwing blackbirds and the (last but not) least bittern, poor thing, have their choice of shoals and breaks to patrol. Watching life in reverential silence on this grey evening would be especially calming but for the invasion of the Lakefield Air Force. I have no repellent.

∾

Lakefield College School boasts soccer and rugby pitches, tennis courts, a stone chapel, boarding houses, a dining hall, a boathouse, a state-of-the-art theatre, manicured lawns and tasteful landscaping – all the accoutrements the rich and wannabe famous could want for their socially networking proteges. How many town girls swooned when Prince Andrew studied here in 1977?

Outside the college's theatre, Lakefield's gentry is decked out in full finery for the festival gala opening. I tighten the laces on my hikers, check my jeans fly and roll up the cuffs of my lumberjack shirt. Inside, the rows of seats fill up with wine-carrying culture vultures while the literary luminaries dance about arm-in-arm in front of the stage for publicity photos. They include Alistair MacLeod; Shelagh Rogers from the CBC; the publisher of *The Walrus* magazine; and tonight's readers, Sheree Fitch and Donna Morrissey.

The lights dim, the crowd shushes and a projector splashes slides of past festival stars onto a huge screen. The audience, eager to declare its sophistication, selects whom to applaud: Shelagh Rogers, June Callwood, Shelagh Rogers, Michael Ondaatje, Peter Gzowski, Shelagh Rogers. Apparently, Shelagh has held down the job of emcee for the past several years.

Though the first reader is no novice, Sheree Fitch plays the student writer worshiping at the feet of Alistair MacLeod. In contrast, Donna Morrissey, introduced by Shelagh as "a spirited woman," prefers the role of brash ball-buster who can make men squirm in their seats when she is slamming her ex, although she did admit to "a certain softening" of their mutual feelings after some time had passed. She is, after all, a Newfoundland girl from an outpost community of twelve houses, and she has carved out an honest persona that will yield no ground to Toronto's pseudo-intellectuals. She, too, acknowledges Alistair as a god, though as far as most people know, he has published but two books of literary merit; one a novel and one a collection of short stories. Alistair, however, is a gentleman's gentleman, an unassailable icon who oozes wisdom with the casual confidence of a Cape Breton fiddler, and always in a manner of humility that Donna Morrissey has yet to learn. Canadian writers from Farley Mowat to Milton Acorn and Al Purdy have known that a persona keeps many doors open. None of this is disingenuous, unless you include excesses like reports of Farley chasing teenage girls about in his tartan kilt at Writers in the School events; it's just a colourful attribute that helps sustain marketability in a thinly populated marketplace.

ↂ

Thus ends my Day in the Life of Lakefield, July 17, 2009. Kudos to the village people for making so much of themselves, for selling their town even to their own citizens. Believing is doing, and these residents are believers. Until you say you are something, how do you know you are? Why would Prince Andrew or Tom Hanks ever come to Lakefield? I wouldn't have, but I'm glad I did.

Now, to find Fire Road 93 in the dark, and my lodgings for the night.

Tips on Photographic Portraiture

Up until last week I was secure in my sexuality. A heterosexual male, short and sweet, though not in the sense you're thinking. Average actually, according to reports from the distaff side, piss hard-ons notwithstanding. And for any dysfunction due to age that may befall me, my imagination is as active as ever and my sex life ultimately healthy, if sometimes minus a partner or a pill.

Then I went to photography class.

It was a special session at the instructor's studio. We learned about "painting with light," building the set from leftover movie "rock" walls to look like a Napa Valley winery showroom, soft focusing to flatter otherwise imperfect skin, posing family members so they would play off each other – and then the penny dropped. It dropped in the form of a helpful hint, a photographer's inside tip, a bonus secret for taking this course from a pro. And it made me look at the world quite differently ever since.

Remember in childhood how we boys would be on watch for the limp-wristed, light-in-the-loafers lisper to scapegoat our own insecurities? Well, turns out we were looking in the wrong direction. There's another telltale sign, known only to photographers, I now believe, and of pecuniary interest to them if they want to get paid for their portrait work. It has to do with how you lean your head, or in what direction. Everybody does it. But which way? Women, I was told, may lean their head in either direction, left or right, according to their whim. Not surprisingly, this reveals nothing about their sexual proclivities. Men, however, are not so serendipitous. According to the expert photographer, heterosexual men lean their head one way and homosexual men, the other. It stands to reason, then, that the photographer had better get the lean correct when posing the subject, or face recriminations and refusal from his client when he sees the results.

My problem, yet another associated with age, is that I have forgotten which way is which. You might think this of little consequence since I do not make my living taking photographs of men. You would be quite wrong. This simple fact has shaken me to the core. If I lean to the left, am I gay? Am I sending signals I have no intention of sending? All these years, have I been sabotaging my attempts to appear at least somewhat attractive to the opposite sex, whatever that might now mean?

Nobody much buys a tailor-made suit anymore, at least not me. But the last time I did, I was asked the executive question, "Do you dress left or right?" I am sure I am not the first to wonder why right- or left-handedness should concern a tailor, but a series of meaningful glances proclaiming messages from "Oh god, here we go again," to "Your dick, idiot, which side?" allowed us to bridge the impasse. But now, after all this, I'm wondering whether there is something to it, right or left. Suppose the big head leans right to counterbalance the little head hanging left, or vice versa? In which case, was that tailor really asking me if I was gay? You see how upsetting this can become.

I find myself watching men seated in front of me in crowded theatres to see if I can ascertain the so-called ten percent leaning one way, so I would know to lean my head the other, but I can't figure it out. To complicate matters, there are a surprisingly large number of men who, like their ladies, switch from side to side. Are they conflicted? Don't they know they are sexually ambiguous? Is this a ruse to see who in the animal kingdom may be attracted to this mating call, this vestigial instinctive behaviour left over from such head-bobbing antics of the horny grebe, for example?

There used to be something about which ear a man wears a single earring in (right if you're gay, then both ears, then the code morphed into fashion and crossed over to straights). Or which pocket he drapes a kerchief out of, though with Springsteen's red ball cap falling out of his right hip pocket on the *Born in the USA* cover – unless he was going for a wider market share – I'm guessing the left hip pocket is the telltale one. Then there's the left/tops, right/bottoms code and, according to Wikipedia, the whole palette of handkerchief colours to advertise one's taste for deviant behaviours. Surely not why Springsteen is "The Boss." It's a minefield, way too dangerous for my addled brain to keep straight, if you'll pardon the pun.

I wonder if I might still be cashing in residuals from post-traumatic stress disorder – that's PTSD, not STD, in case you're thinking I'm a total libertine. The trauma happened sometime in my adolescence, in a darkened movie theatre on Ottawa Street, the one that ran continuous porn from noon to midnight. Right when I'm starting to get a chub on, a man sits down next to me, arranges his trench coat carefully across his lap and slides a hand under it onto my knee. I panic.

I shoot up, stumble down the row of empty seats to the far aisle (in such theatres, patrons space themselves out for obvious reasons) and march up the ramp and out the doors into the bright sunlit smog and stench of the Hammer's east end, where there are no perverts. It cured me from skipping school in the afternoon.

But why did he target me? Had he approached other vulnerable victims on former occasions? Was I the only first-timer there, broadcasting naïveté in my nervous attempt to go unnoticed? Or, I must now ask, was I tilting my head to the wrong side? And if so, why?

Now, I could posit that ten percent of my friends are gay, but one hundred percent of my current friends can be counted on the fingers of both hands, so that would make one gay friend, and I'm sure that's an underestimation. And even if it's not, since I don't know which one, it doesn't let me off the hook, does it?

I've resorted to staring into the mirror for long periods of time, in a manner I haven't done since puberty. Now, instead of searching for blackheads, I'm searching for The Answer. Of course, the reverse image staring back at me isn't helpful. Or perhaps it is. Perhaps we all have a reverse image tilting at its own windmills. Meanwhile, anyway, I'll stay behind the camera.

Love Slips In

at three in the morning
while the world sleeps
gulls cry
a hundred years in each scream

a woman made me cry
she said *I love you*
and was not waiting to be loved

I heard myself
and shook

love slips in with ease
like a boy's face against
cat fur

I touch my boy's cheek
he is always awake

love seeps around one's soul
getting used to it
sifting the alchemy
to turn water to

fire

you could taste the flames
watch them underlight the crest
of cheekbones
haze her in gold
of Elvira Madigan

before she was shot by her lover

you might have thought the fire
was blood
flowing between us

so it began
like a pearl round a grain of sand
a marriage round an entreaty

beautiful as letters in a word
as blue flame leaping from end veins

beautiful is first love
newly arrived to old friends

our fingers sang in chorus
orchestrating leaps and falls
and smooth hellos
as though they were the last survivors
and had never met

no one thought to tell me
she had gone
and I had not heard her burning

space crowded with certainties
private places on beaches
children wet with laughter
a chance to touch her shoulder
crowded with her

as clear
as the land
suddenly
illuminated by lightning

Return of the Perseids

"The ways we miss our lives are life."
— Randall Jarrell, "A Girl in the Library," *The Seven-League Crutches*

Not tropic nor temperate
love casts aside the safe days
leaves us to ourselves
a reckoned danger.

One August night
we caught sky streakers
in our hands like fireflies
and released them
back to the stuck stars.

Winter's last sundown
I run to your window –
the candles out,
your face nestled in feathers.

I scuff my feet
on the gravel shoulder,
and search out of season
for those star children
that blazed a path to greet us.

Haida Gwaii

The reasons for my trip to the Queen Charlotte Islands, now known as Haida Gwaii (as the Haida nation has always called them), are deep and varied.

When I immigrated to Canada from England at the age of eight and a half, I soon found that what I was didn't count here. My good academic record quickly went south when my spelling suffered from being unable to decipher the teacher's accent or to replace my upright British script for the loopy slanted alphabet posted above the chalkboards. On the playground, I could hit a cricket ball on the ground but not a baseball in mid-air; I could kick a soccer ball but not throw a football; and, of course, I had never worn skates. In a rural Ontario school in 1953, ten years before the Beatles jumped the pond, my English accent sounded sissified and was the subject of ridicule. All of this made me unfit for this country, a sensibility I suspect most immigrants bear for years. The "adapt or die" principle kicked in quickly and I survived as a stranger in this strange land, where my first Canadian friend was named Boris Wanechko, his nationality unknown to me to this day. I had come to Canada as a schoolboy who played cowboys and Indians and expected snowbound logging camps and red-coated policemen on horseback, namely Sergeant Preston of the Yukon, and I had found a place where I did not belong.

Years later in 1970, as a high school English teacher developing one of Ontario's first courses in CanLit, I came across Douglas LePan's poem "A Country Without a Mythology." In it, a European paddler canoes a Canadian wilderness river dreaming in vain of his familiar archetypal images – the abbey clock, the garden sundial – while, unseen by him, deep in the bush, "teeters some lust-red manitou." I wanted to meet the manitou.

155

In 1980 I travelled to the Sunshine Coast and stayed with friends, Leigh and Clarke, deep in the forest in their self-built log home without any public utilities or services. I slept in the cedar shack Clarke had lived in while he crafted the house from trees cut down where the house now stood, two circular towers and a third taller one still under construction, its tree logs notched together by chainsaw artistry. During the day, I helped him fell trees for the supply of winter firewood. The BC wilderness drew on my imagination and emotions and led to profound questioning.

My father understood his world by interpreting two paradigms, the biblical and the botanical. Sometimes this led to a force-fit of evidences, but it sustained him through doubt and difficulty. I have tended to polarize the two, and if I lack a spiritual dimension to my life, I shall likely seek it in nature first. This is what led me to the Queen Charlottes.

In July of 2004, I sat beside a working logger on the small plane from Vancouver to Prince Rupert and across to Haida Gwaii. We chatted about logging, his view being that clear-cutting causes no permanent damage to the forests, as we could see from the sky. From this height, the forests look like distant golf courses, the clear-cuts simply fairways quickly carpeted green from millions of seeds the forest holds in its soil. Tree planting is done to ensure second-growth forest and to appease the activists, he said, but it is not necessary. The American company that bought out MacMillan Bloedel, Weyerhauser, gets everything they want; that is, "everything America wants. Logging and fishing has sustained the economy of islanders since the whites first settled here, but neither will survive the mismanagement that has robbed working people of their livelihood." He did not mention that what has been harvested from the old-growth forests will never exist again – thousand-year-old monumental trees in the richest pristine sanctuary for wildlife north of the Galapagos Islands.

The Haida have all the rights to the best trees, he continued, which they mark and damage by stripping bark for weaving and drilling holes to test for a hollow core, which makes them unsuitable for carving.

This renders the trees "culturally modified," a legal term that forbids their destruction by logging. I asked whether the Haida were accepting of white tourists. He said in general they are a sociable lot, but some of them up in Old Massett would sooner fight than talk. He had no ill feelings towards them; he just stayed away from those few people. His past girlfriend was Haida, so he couldn't possibly be in any way prejudiced, he assured me.

The ocean suddenly rose up to meet us, and at the last moment was replaced by the aptly named Sandspit airstrip. Inside the terminal, I was intrigued by a hollowed-out fourteen-foot canoe paddled from Alaska to the top of Graham Island by Mary Carey, the wife of Neil Carey, who had written the guide book I had been studying. Outside, meanwhile, the "airport limousine," an off-season school bus, had quietly picked up passengers and left for the Alliford Bay ferry. I was stranded at the airport in the rain, on South Moresby Island, miles from the last ferry of the day, which should have taken me to Graham Island and my hotel in Queen Charlotte City.

I was not alone. Also in my predicament was a graduate student named Anthony. Together, we rang for the only taxi on the island, which was, of course, in use. The driver agreed to let us join her party, and with a drop-off on the way, we arrived at the ferry terminal in time to see the boat approaching. Anthony spotted a van in the queue with the lettering *Queen Charlotte Adventures*, the name of the tour company that would take us to the old abandoned Haida villages on the southern, largely inaccessible Gwaii Haanas National Park Island. I learned right then that one's plans change as often as they are made on the Charlottes, but things work out anyway.

Next day, our group set out from Spruce Point Lodge in Charlotte (Queen Charlotte City) for Camp Moresby. There we boarded our transportation for the week, a small craft powered by two 250-horse engines worth $18,000 apiece that rattled and clattered and slammed us down onto the Pacific with such force that we thought either the boat's sheathing or our bones would come loose. Captain James Kidd, who had sailed his own boat up from Vancouver through a large school of two hundred porpoises a few days before, stood at the helm. His buddy Glenn, our blond and braided guide and cook, lashed down the gas cans and supplies. Both looked like college kids on a summer junket, too young to inspire much confidence. The others on our great adventure were Frank, the Aussie, and his friend Wilson, the children's lawyer and sketch artist; Maurice and Lucie, French-speaking Ontarians; Anthony, the Sri Lankan student; and me. We few, we happy few, drawn to explore this little-known paradise.

The abandoned village sites, accessible only by water, are guarded by Watchmen, Haida men and women who volunteer to act as guides and protectors of their cultural heritage. It's the evening of Day Two, and I've unrolled my sleeping bag on the floor of a Haida longhouse, part of a youth camp at Swan Bay. Today we toured T'anuu, a village of five hundred fifty Haida who either died from smallpox or evacuated to the larger centres at Skidegate and Massett to escape the pox. Foundations of the houses lie in ruins, overgrown by moss. One house with a tunnelled entrance belonged to a chief who would invite the leaders of warring tribes to his potlatch. A warrior with a sharpened knife-spear would lop off the head of the guest as he bent low through the entrance, while the chief's people celebrated inside, sending up a howl to cover the noise of the killing.

The ruins are massive, eerily silent and compelling in the rainforest's reclamation of them. A decaying mortuary board, which once masked the burial boxes of two important Haida warriors, now stares out at the sky with blank eyes. I asked the Watchman if he finds the place spiritual and he said, "Yes. Sometimes something will happen, like I feel someone touch me on the shoulder, but I turn and no one is there." He asked his partner if she found it so, and she said no, she only hates the rats. As for myself, I fought back tears, a reaction that surprised me and yet seemed appropriate also. There are ghosts here.

Haida society is matrilineal, divided into two moieties, Raven and Eagle. A Haida's moiety derives from the mother. Someone asked the old Watchman if he was related to every Haida on the islands. He thought about it and said, "Well, we were seven thousand; seven hundred after smallpox, and the two thousand born after them. A Raven must marry an Eagle and an Eagle must marry a Raven, so yes, I probably am related to everyone on the islands."

Haida artist Bill Reid revisited his Haida heritage later in his life. His portrayals of Haida creation myths and symbology in cedar, jade and bronze grace the Canadian Embassy in Washington, DC; Vancouver's airport and aquarium; and our $20 bill. The Watchman at S'kang Gway told me of his mother's mother, who knew Bill Reid's mother. The woman lived to be one hundred two years old. When Bill died in 1998, fourteen Haida paddled his magnificent fifty-foot red cedar dugout war canoe, *Loo Taas* – which means "wave-eater" – two days up the Pacific coast to T'anuu, his mother's village. They carried his remains in a bentwood box to be buried there with a stone marker that says simply, "In Memory Iljuwas Yalth Sgwansang," his Haida name. The old woman cried. The Watchman, one of the paddlers who had paddled the canoe backwards into the old village site, asked his nonny (grandmother) why she was crying. She said it was the first time she had ever seen a war canoe approach a village backwards, in peace.

I found that canoe housed in a carver's shed in Skidegate. Another one of its paddlers, Andy Wilson, was teaching a young apprentice the art of painting a paddle when I visited. He told me how the canoe was made, first by shaping the bow and stern and then by taking out the inside wood, each carver working on a small section and knowing to stop when he scraped the pins driven in from the outside to indicate thickness. Then, on a windless day, water was poured into the canoe and boiled with fire rocks to limber the wood, the weight of the water pushing out the sides to accept the seat planks. Bill painted the sides with killer whale and human forms, which flow from prow to stern.

159

Next door, I met master carver Robert Vosgard, whose brother was killed in a logging accident three years before. Since his brother was Raven, Robert was carving a short pole with Raven clan images to honor him. The wood was his brother's fish-cleaning block. He said it was full of fish oil and blood, as well as some of his brother's blood.

In dense first-growth forest accessible only by logging roads near Juskatla, I stumble across a fifty-foot Haida canoe partially carved and then abandoned where it lay. The Haida used these ocean-going vessels to trade sea otter pelts for iron, post-contact. Either the people died of smallpox before finishing this one, or they discovered the wood unfit to continue and moved on. I run my hand along the marks the adze made as the brown workman leaned his back into the cut. This was the effort of survival. How much did he extract from the bulk before he knew the canoe that hid inside the tree would never emerge as seaworthy?

A Watchman later told me he knows of six such abandoned canoes on the islands. I asked him how they would get them out of the forest. He said they would wait for winter and sled them out on the snow, which still seems an impossibility to me given the terrain and forestation. He said they would fell a huge tree by lighting two fires, one on each side, and setting alder saplings upright against the trunk to gage the burn. When one side's sapling bent, they would put mud on its fire and stoke the opposite fire to burn more of the other side. When both fires burned into the trunk evenly and the tree bent both saplings, a man would go up the trunk past the flare and notch the tree to make it fall exactly where they wanted it to.

On the way back to Misty Meadows Campground in Naikoon Provincial Park, I hiked a trail through some gigantic first-growth trees. I stood inside the hollow trunk of a cedar and craned my neck to see where the sinews of wood disappeared into darkness. This trail used to end at a golden spruce tree, the subject of John Vaillant's brilliant book *The Golden Spruce*. It was cut down in protest by a mainlander who had come to the islands for work and was disliked by many and fired by his employer. The unique tree was yellow because its leaves lacked chlorophyll, and it figures in Haida mythology. The vilified man fled to the mainland, bragged of his deed, was caught and was set to be tried in Massett, back on Haida Gwaii. To assure himself the publicity he craved, he announced to the press that he would paddle from Rupert to Massett in a kayak. His kayak was found bashed in, with no trace of him. Was he wrecked, was he murdered, or did he stage his escape? The University of British Columbia sent their horticultural people to study the fallen spruce and take cuttings before it met its demise. They since have donated saplings to the Haida, who have planted a new golden spruce behind a chain-link cage in the church memorial garden in Port Clements.

Old Massett is a Haida reserve, with house clan and mortuary poles in front of homes, the school, the community centre, St. John's Haida Church, the baseball field and a Haida art shop. Behind one house with a house pole is a large carver's shed. Inside, in various degrees of completion, are one huge totem pole, five canoes, a row of painted paddles, a mask with white fur trim and a house-front design. Clarence, the carver, has gone for lunch. Seeing the living work completes my journey. A Haida man outside says to me, "Some good things in there." I ask him where the pole will go. "Over there," he says, pointing to a house nearby. This magnificent work is staying in Old Massett, made by Haida carvers for the Haida Nation. No more traders, anthropologists, museum curators, wealthy collectors, government agencies, robbers of any stripe. These aboriginals are rebuilding their culture. Their houses are still shabby, the vacant ones sometimes windowless. Their youth can have all their education paid for, but most drop out. Alcohol and drugs are huge problems. Government money has built new longhouse meeting halls, band council buildings, schools like longhouse mansions, and yet the local newspaper reports that the reserve is over $2,000,000 in debt, mostly because of misappropriation of funds and too many people employed on government money. Hope, however, lies with the dancers and storytellers and carvers and weavers, the artists rediscovering and reinterpreting their story. They learn the old ways from the masters, and build the new with those tools. Robert Davidson says he can name any carver on the islands by the signature way he cuts the ovoids.

My stay is nearing its end. I'm sitting beside the wreck of the *Pezuta*, a barge that ran aground on East Beach in 1928. All that remains visible is the bow stubbornly thrusting up from the hard sand. This beach is eighty kilometres long, and the only other human I've seen today just passed me on a bicycle. The tide is coming in. I can't stay here because this half-mile-wide beach will soon disappear and I could get trapped on a sandspur. The hike here is five kilometres each way – part river trail, part forest and part beach. On the way, at the mouth of the river, I stop to watch a couple of sea otters frolic in the setting sun. In a clearing near the river bank stands a deserted fisherman's shake cabin, with floats, lines and nets sprawled across the front porch, the winter's firewood stacked around one side, a boat leaning upright against a tree and a nearby vegetable garden picket-fenced to keep out the deer. The deer are small, not by breed alone but because they are too plentiful and kill off the vegetation that sustains them. The locals don't hunt them, they "go shopping." The scene is classic pioneer, a place "of come and gone," as Earle Birney wrote.

On my last morning, I had a fish and shrimp wrap at the Sea Raven, my favourite eatery on the islands, with Mary and her Spruce Point Lodge gang. I hadn't seen them since I'd left the boat a week ago. She spoke of the expensive repairs to the engine, whose gear was stripped when we travelled to Ninstints, the Unesco World Heritage site. Captain Kidd had proven his mettle that night by rigging a temporary fix while we slept. "BOAT means Bring Out Another Ten thousand," Mary joked.

At the ferry landing, I met the Sandspit taxi driver who saved Anthony and I from being stranded at the airport back at the beginning of all this. She said the only time the power goes out these days is when an eagle has flown into the wires. On the route across the bay, I watched the land's changing outlines from the ship rail, savouring every last minute in the presence of Haida Gwaii, Islands of The People.

Flying Air Canada's redeye through the night from Vancouver to Toronto, we pass an electrical storm over some western city. Lightning lights it up like Iraq's first night of war. Then, the finishing touch – a whole journey across this country accompanied by the aurora borealis to the north, outside my window. Its sweeps and curves and verticals shimmer in and out of the darkness, immense from my view above the clouds, filling the whole northern horizon and reaching up to paint a quarter of the canopy's expanse with light. I am watching the inspiration for Haida artists. The other passengers sleep through this blessing.

Back home, eagles don't fly into our hydro wires. We don't honour our loved ones and our ancestors by carving the crests of their lineage in poles of unparalleled beauty and stature. We would not blockade a logging road as Bill Reid and Guujaaw, President of the Council of the Haida Nation, did on Lyell Island, forcing a government to turn a whole rainforest into a protected national park and a ghost town into a World Heritage site. And if a plague inflicted upon us by a conquering nation wiped out all but one in ten of us, would we look to the arts to restore our life and dignity? Would we create our way out of the darkness? I've seen more gentleness, more respect, more reverence for life in the people of Haida Gwaii, native and white, than I've seen anywhere.

Did I meet the lust-red manitou I sought? If not, then I walked in the places where he lives. I touched his totems and read in their carved eyes his story of creation and loss, of death and spirit life, of war and love. I saw his people living beside their murderers, making myths for their days, myths that could sustain us all. I felt his hand clinging even now to the land. I heard his voice sing and watched his body dance.

The traffic closes in. I feel changed. I have to get used to belonging here again. I am home. Yet I am still a visitor, trying to find my way in this country, which has become my own land. The question is not Margaret Atwood's "Where is here?" but "Who am I, here?" A village, a city, a landscape, a civilization – we are all visitors seeking our place on this planet, where we may find ourselves. I recall Rudy Wiebe writing about a northern people: "We have no word in our language that means 'wilderness', as everywhere we go is our home."

Whale

we set out upon the northern sea
as though it were a backwater
our blades tearing at the swells
like spawning salmon
our hearts full of war

alongside the gunwale
the great shadow exploded
up and over our heads
a weightless leviathan
its eye cast down upon us
and lunged back into the sea
and sounded

the wake of its flukes
did not swamp us
nor deter us
from our course
though our drum skin
did not tremble
and we paddled
quiet as the deeps

Bear

In the dimming orange light of sunset, I arrive by logging road at an isolated clearing on the West's wild coast. I set up camp. A few yards from my tent, I see a bear's scat, identifiable by the twist at one end of the turd. That night, I leave the car door unlocked. Next morning, I see what had attracted the bear. At the edge of the site is a make-shift plank table, stained dark with fish oil. Skeletons and heads of salmon and halibut loll in the surf. Sport fishermen, I guess, clean their catch here. A Haida Watchman will tell me later that tourists, mostly Americans, are helicoptered to a remote pier at the mouth of the sound where they board a schooner that plies these waters and harvests their spoils. Happy to be higher on the food chain than fish scraps, I breathe a sigh of relief, pack my tent and drive back up the slippery gravel road. Not a hundred yards from my campsite, on a steep incline dangerously channeled by rains, I spot him.

Bear, almost as large as a grizzly, is an island black born on Haida Gwaii. Healthier than those in the rest of Canada, he harvests the moveable feast of berries and fish the gods provide in season.

Bear goes where I cannot. I cannot eat his food or tread his unmarked paths or sleep in his den.

Bear walked through my campsite the day before. His scat is still soft though no longer steaming. His giant footprint in the mud is filled with water. The fish oil on the cleaning board and the halibut carcass at the water's edge explain his visit.

Bear lopes easily across the logging road. We meet each other at right angles. "Oh, yes!" I shout in the cabin of my car. His back is higher than my car's roof, his stride longer than my car's width, his massive head greater than my car window, his jaws able to crunch through my torso had he been hungry.

When Bear crosses the road, his paws touch down but twice on the gravel strip cut wide enough for logging trucks to pass each other. Two more steps, the crashing fades. The forest swallows him. I have seen only one human run through the undergrowth like this, leaping from log to log as though he had been raised among the cumbrous rotting trunks and moss-covered clutter of the rainforest floor. Glenn, our striking young guide with the swagger of a seaman, led me into an old-growth forest on Gwaii Haanas a week before. Had he taken care to tread safely, like a man crossing over thin ice, he likely would have fallen, his legs twisted and trapped in the weave of decaying undergrowth, his hesitation inevitably conquering his spirit. Yet, when he posed for my camera at the base of a giant Douglas fir, he looked a mere child in his red rain shell and wellies.

My words do not name what it is to be Bear. My shortcomings as a sentient being sharing this planet keep the distance wide between Bear and me. Bear is everything I am not. Bear is the persistence of an inchworm traversing a thousand-year-old log. Bear is the life that recedes inside the dormant maple. Bear is unknowable.

Our relationship is fleeting, merely one of address. As he disappears from my view, Bear does not look back.

The Feather

Nearing the end of my trip to Haida Gwaii, I stopped by the Naikoon Park headquarters. Naikoon Provincial Park takes up the whole northeast corner of Graham Island, including ninety-five kilometres of northern and eastern beaches and 170,000 acres of forested land. I had already climbed the volcanic core of Tow Hill and spied Alaska from the most northern beach, Rose Spit.

Sunday morning, the park office was closed. On the railing of the large deck likely used for instructional purposes, someone had left a jar containing eagle feathers.

Before I left home, I had promised an eagle feather to my six-year-old grandson. He collected Pokémon cards and model cars, but also exotic shells and lake stones. I thought he might value a feather, especially since there were no bald eagles in our area at the time. Perhaps he might find a connection to Native culture if I helped him to understand what the eagle feather can mean.

I had already found several smaller ones lying about on the beaches of Haida Gwaii, likely body feathers dislodged by preening or pushed out during molting. They looked less impressive than our seagull feathers back home. This jar, however, contained many feathers, all of a size that would astonish a child or adult unfamiliar with the birds they came from. I drew one out and admired it: a primary wing feather, dark grey-brown, about eighteen inches long, with a thick quill and a small tuft of white down at the base of the perfectly aligned vanes. I gently pulled one of the vanes apart and then smoothed it back together from bottom to top. I packed the feather in tissue and a mailing tube and tied it onto my backpack. My grandson would be happy.

If the Americans had not adopted the bald eagle as their national symbol, though they didn't remove it from the endangered list until

2007, I expect Canadians gladly would have retired our amphibious rodent in favour of the majestic raptor.

In my youth, I read the Sunday lesson from a Bible that rested on the outspread polished brass wings of an eagle at my church. More recently, I was passed an eagle feather in a smudging ceremony to celebrate the summer solstice on Aboriginal Day in Gage Park, Hamilton. The eagle can look into the face of the sun, as Christ can look into the face of the Father.

Witnesses at the inquiry into the killing of Dudley George testified with an eagle feather in their hand. Elijah Harper clasped an eagle feather when he said "No" to the Meech Lake Accord in 1990. A man in the gallery of the House of Commons held an eagle feather aloft for over an hour when Prime Minister Harper apologized for the residential schools in 2008.

Honour, strength, respect, wisdom, achievement, leadership – all these are represented by the eagle feather. What grandfather would not wish to instill these in his grandson? My eagle feather would stand for integrity, for the harmonious confluence of right thinking and attendant action. I couldn't hold an eagle feather and lie. I couldn't give an eagle feather that I had taken without asking.

Back home, I placed this magnificent feather above a picture of Bear Mother by Walker Brown from Skidegate, which he had made for a poster decrying the bear kills. This most respectful of tourists had turned out to be one more lying pillager at heart, the sacred feather one more trophy.

Some days later, my grandson saw it and asked to have it. I denied him. That afternoon, I anonymously mailed it with a sheepishly apologetic note back to the Naikoon Park Office, in the same mailing tube which had brought it home.

I did not know that I could have been convicted, fined up to $5000 and jailed for one year for possessing and transporting any part of an eagle. Nor that I could never take a feather, buy one, sell one or give one away to my grandson without breaking laws like the Bald Eagle Protection Act of 1940 – laws that protect migratory birds whether threatened with extinction or not. Nor that eagle carcasses are sent to the National Eagle Repository in a secure military facility in the Rocky Mountains of Colorado and their parts released only to a long waiting list of certified status Indians from government-recognized tribes for strictly cultural, religious or ceremonial functions. I would learn later that fifty birds were found slaughtered by traffickers on a North Vancouver beach in 2006. A single feather can fetch a hundred dollars on the black market – a whole carcass, thousands – because the powwow circuit awards hefty financial prizes to dancers with the best costumes, which usually means those with the most feathers. My ignorance of the law would not have argued against my guilt. By giving the feather to my six-year-old grandson, I unknowingly would have criminalized him also.

With the taking of that feather, I had joined with the logger who, on orders from the company, cut down and moved a Haida potlatch pole at Skedans to clear a passage for the transport of logs by water. I had joined with the lumberjack who sat beside me on the plane from Rupert to Sandspit and claimed that the forest heals itself when denuded by his clear-cutting. I had joined the sailors from centuries ago who took away sea otter pelts and left behind smallpox that all but wiped out a nation. I am the reason the Haida Watchmen guard their sites. We are all in need of a healing circle.

Acknowledgements

Several of the works in this book have appeared in the following journals, books, and websites:

Journals: *Canadian Forum, The Windsor Review, Great Lakes Review, Dream Catcher, Canadian Author & Bookman, Canadian Teacher, Hammered Out, Origins, Grey Borders.*

Books: *Reclamation* (Borealis Press, 1980); *Voices of Niagara* (Moonstone Press, 1980); *Saving Bannister* (Canadian Authors Association, Niagara, 2011); *The Fruits of Experience* (Emanation Press, 1979).

Websites: ditchpoetry.com, canadianteachermagazine.com

I am grateful to the following people who influenced this book: Don Mackenzie, my first reader and honest critic; Noelle Allen, my publisher and editor, who shaped a book out of the shreds and patches I submitted; the staff at Wolsak and Wynn, who copy-edited the manuscript; dear friends and family who appear as characters in these pages and enrich my life with their surprising love and loyalty; and Shirl, my wife, for leaving me alone to write and for being there when I stop.

I came along at a fortuitous time when the brightest and best in Canadian literature made themselves available to the public. I took my students to see the likes of Atwood, Purdy, Birney, Laurence, Acorn, Mowat, Mitchell, nichol and bissett. When I caught the writing bug, I sought instruction not from teachers but from writers. Whether through a course, a summer workshop or a twelve-hour monthly session in my mentor's apartment, I received an enviable apprenticeship that served both my writing and my teaching well. Though there are also others, I want to thank especially Joe Rosenblatt, Matt Cohen,

John Herbert and Austin Clarke for their generosity, tutelage and professional friendship. Their patient caring about the scribbling of a novice should not go unrecognized.

David Haskins emigrated from England to Beamsville, ON, in 1953 at the age of eight, and now lives in Grimsby with his wife and his 1970 MGB. He holds an Honours B.A. in English from McMaster University and a M.Ed. from University of Toronto. His teaching career spans thirty-five years, mostly in secondary schools with five as the Department Head of English. Haskins also taught correspondence courses in writing and journalism for the Ontario Ministry of Education and at Brock University. Other writings include a creative writing text, theatre reviews for a Toronto arts newspaper and memoir pieces. He is currently preparing books of recent poems and short stories, and a children's fantasy novel.